THE UNSPOKEN TRUTH ABOUT RELIGION

The Unspoken TRUTH About Religion

Dick Johnson

Cover photo: Statue of Jesus weeping in Oklahoma City

Copyright © 2018 Dick Johnson
All rights reserved.

ISBN-10: 198381413X
ISBN-13: 9781983814136
Library of Congress Control Number: 2018901681
CreateSpace Independent Publishing Platform
North Charleston, South Carolina

Contents

Preface · ix
Introduction · xi

1 The Vital Nature of Truth · 1
  - Our Ultimate Common Denominator · · · · · · · · · · · · · · · 2
  - Essential to Learning and Achieving · · · · · · · · · · · · · · · · 2
  - Consciously Grasping the Concept of Truth · · · · · · · · · 4
  - What Determines Our Relationship with Truth · · · · · · · · 4
  - Truth's Dependence on Rationality · · · · · · · · · · · · · · · · · 5
  - The Instinctual Process of Determining Truth · · · · · · · · · 7
  - Development of This Unconscious Capability · · · · · · · · 9
  - The Natural Effects of Determining
    Truth Subconsciously · 10
  - The Boundless Possibilities of Determining
    Truth Ourselves · 11
2 The Limited and Limiting Role of Our Senses · · · · · · · · · · · · 14
3 How Information from Our Senses Becomes
  Our Behaviors · 17
  - We Are a Species of Animal · 17
  - The Essential Function of Our Emotions · · · · · · · · · · · · · 18
  - Life Is All About How We Feel · 21

- The Irresistible Allure of Our Genetic Guidance ····· 22
- The Distorting Effects of Our Genetic Guidance ····· 22
- Our Innate Discomfort with the Unknown ··········· 24
- Our Disproportionate Aversion to Detriment········· 24

4 Nature's Exceptionless Mandate
That We Benefit Ourselves ························· 26
- Our Two Basic and Mutually Exclusive Types
  of Benefit··································· 29
- Our Perpetual Dilemma of Truth vs. Acceptance ····· 33
- The Seductive Illusion of Selflessness ············· 35
- The Nature Behind Good and Bad Behaviors ········ 36
- When Our Need for Acceptance Becomes
  Secondary·································· 38

5 The Ever-Present Influence of Our Unconscious
Associations······································ 41

6 Our Incredibly Useful and Occasionally
Lethal Imagination ······························· 46

7 Our Comforting Misperceptions
of Conscious Choice and Free Will ·················· 51

8 The Role of Conscious Thought in Determining Our
Behaviors······································· 54
- The Spawning of Conscious Thought··············· 54
- The Irrational Push of Our Emotions to Skip
  Conscious Thought···························· 56

9 Nature in Our Relationships ······················· 63
- It's All About the Benefits We Receive ············· 63
- Our Qualities and Traits Have a Market Value ········ 64
- When the Benefits Go Not To Ourselves, But
  To Our Species······························· 66

- 10 Belief vs. Self-delusion, Our Most Harmful Confusion · · · 68
  - The Categorical Difference between a Belief and a Self-delusion · 68
  - Why Absolutely No One Believes In God · · · · · · · · · · · · 71
  - How Self-delusion Can Be So Harmful · · · · · · · · · · · · · 73
  - Recognizing Our Self-delusions · · · · · · · · · · · · · · · · · · 76
- 11 Our Exclusively Human Thirst for Religion · · · · · · · · · · · · · 79
  - What Religion Does for Us · 80
  - The Genesis of Religion · 81
  - Why Religious Views Change Over Time · · · · · · · · · · · · 82
  - How and Why Religion and Reason Are Mutually Exclusive · 83
  - When We Infer Knowledge from What We Do Not Know · 86
  - The Original Intent of a Christian Nation · · · · · · · · · · · · 89
  - Our Government's Implicit Endorsement of Religion · · · 90
  - Religion amongst the Foibles of Our Supreme Court · · · 93
  - The Immeasurable Importance of Separating Church and State · 97
  - All Religions Are Equally Invalid · · · · · · · · · · · · · · · · · · 99
  - Religion's Dependence on Self-delusion · · · · · · · · · · · 100
  - Pascal's Ill-conceived Wager · 104
  - Religion – Spiritual Snake Oil for Ailing Values and Morals · 105
  - What Actually Shapes Our Values and Morality · · · · · · 110
  - The Problem with Atheists Is They Present No Problem · 111
  - Pulling Back the Curtain on How Religion Actually Affects Our Behavior · · · · · · · · · · · · · · · · · · 113

- The Many Ways Religion Generates Harm ·········· 116
- How Religion Undermines the Precious Nature of Life ································ 122
- Our Unwitting Complicity in Religious Conflicts the World Over ···················· 124
- A Significant Interim Moral Question ·············· 126

12 The Costly Divisive Effects of Not Understanding Human Behavior ································ 127

13 Our Growing Awareness ························· 131
- Our Unrelenting Migration from Irrational to Rational Behaviors ······························ 134
- How Our Growing Awareness Is Gradually Dissolving Religion ···························· 136
- The Unrivaled Significance of Rational vs. Irrational Behaviors ·································· 139

14 Twelve Elemental Truths and the Global Peace That Awaits Their Recognition ···················· 142

15 A Footnote of Sorts about Our Subjective Perspective ······································ 148

Notes ··· 149
List of Quotes ····································· 159

Preface

If I had to sum up my life's perspective in two words, they would probably be "Yeah, but..." It seems no matter where I go or what I do, I find myself advocating for the things that never get said. I recall once taking part in a friendly lunchtime discussion about politics. When it was over, the liberals thought I was a conservative and the conservatives thought I was a liberal. All because I asked about the things they had each conveniently failed to mention. Granted, it's only natural to argue just our own side in any debate. But when we don't have a side, when all we seek is truth and understanding, we naturally want the whole story, which it seems rarely gets told. In the words of 18th-century German philosopher Johann Georg Hamann, "A thirsty ambition for truth and virtue, and a frenzy to conquer all lies and vices which are not recognized as such nor desire to be; herein consists the heroic spirit of the philosopher."[1]

My intent with this book is to spotlight many of the uncomfortable truths that routinely get left out of our conversations, chief among them being the actual reasons we practice religion. At some point, whether we are religious or not, we each question religious precepts, whether there is a God, whether we believe, whether we should believe. But unlike with any other human behavior, there has been no objective source that we can turn to for factual answers regarding religion, a state of affairs that has fostered our greatest falsehoods and led to our deadliest conflicts. By answering every conceivable question regarding religion, more often than not in categorical terms, this book fills that critical void. And while it utilizes science and empirical data to prove them, the observations and conclusions this book presents are not a product of academic study or even mainstream thinking; they have been garnered from everyday experiences, which means that there is likely nothing in here that you do not already know at the subconscious level, just a lot of important realities that have yet to emerge as conscious knowledge.

Introduction

Religion is held to be the source of our values and morals, the impetus behind all things good. Yet it sustains an unparalleled acquaintance with death, destruction, and terrorism. And generation after generation we fail to acknowledge, much less explore, this glaring incongruity. Historians have written endlessly on the many origins of religion, and critics have written countless volumes on the immeasurable atrocities committed in its name. But here we are in the 21st century splicing genes and colliding particles at near the speed of light, and we still don't have a coherent understanding of why we practice this most enigmatic of human behaviors. We have become aware enough to recognize that a correlation exists between religion and conflict, but not aware enough to grasp how and why.

To understand religion, or any behavior for that matter, we must understand the two elemental components that determine our behaviors: our human nature, which is shaped by genetic instruction, and truth, the reality that all life must discern to survive. By illuminating nature's influence on our behaviors this book doesn't just explain and debunk a great many myths and misconceptions regarding religion, it advances a universal understanding of human behavior.

1

The Vital Nature of Truth

Intrinsic to every religion is the requirement that its followers embrace its tenets as truth. The inherent problem being, every religion has tenets that differ and conflict with every other, making it impossible for all religions to be representing truth. The undeniable reality being, a great many people are deluding themselves with false notions of truth, which of course leads to conflict. For this reason, I felt it would be good to start with a clear understanding of this most basic of terms: truth.

Unfortunately, if truth isn't our most misused word, it's certainly in the top ten. This is why we sometimes feel the need to spell it with a capital T. We have misused the word so often with such colloquial phrases as *my truth* or *your truth* that we must now distinguish when we want to communicate its actual meaning. Just to be clear, when I use the word truth in this book, I am referring to its most literal definition, accordance with fact or reality, which is not subject to anyone's awareness, perspective, or emotional needs.

When we think of truth we generally think in terms of whether or not someone is telling the truth. But truth is not limited to human usage. By definition, it represents the actual state of all things. This is the difference between truth and honesty. Truth is absolute and exists independent of mankind, while honesty represents our limited desire and ability to employ truth.

OUR ULTIMATE COMMON DENOMINATOR

Conventional wisdom among the scientific community is that if we ever encounter intelligent life from another world, we will almost certainly first communicate through math. The reason is that math is entirely objective and factual; it's an entire language of nothing but truth, which means that no matter where you're from or how you communicate, it ensures the same conclusions. This is the fundamental significance of truth. It represents reality, which makes it our ultimate common denominator. Because truth embodies no variance, duplication, or conflict, it serves to ensure agreement and preclude conflict. This is why our goal should never be to have others see things as we do, but rather to offer what we can in a collective effort to realize the truth. When the objective is truth, because everyone is pursuing the exact same thing, there are no adversarial roles. The considerable caveat being, because we are subjective beings, we must each discern truth through a perspective that has been uniquely distorted to satisfy our individual emotional needs.

ESSENTIAL TO LEARNING AND ACHIEVING

As the 17th-century English mathematician and physicist Isaac Newton once stated, "A man may imagine things that are false, but he can only understand things that are true."[2] Such is the essential role of truth in the life of conscious beings. Because understanding is merely the apprehension of reality, truth is essential to all learning and achieving. It is the elemental quality that makes information useful, something perhaps best demonstrated by the sciences, mankind's systematic effort to apply only truths to various fields of study. Because such applied use of truth is the only means we have of achieving a desirable result more often than just random events, the sciences are indispensable in our pursuit of survival.

The fact that truth is essential to our survival is why it means so much to us in our relationships. We instinctively gauge the quality and value of our relationships by the other person's ability and willingness to provide truth. This is why it's so fundamentally important to be truthful with our children. Because children instinctively perceive a parent's willingness to provide truth as a measure of how much they are loved and valued, it exerts considerable influence on their developing self-worth. Unfortunately, when it comes to our children, we all too often find truth inconvenient, leaving our children to eventually perceive that we have denied them a precious commodity during a crucial time, more often than not for our own comfort. This is the essence of how a child loses trust in and respect for a parent. It is the natural result of such unconscious devaluations in their relationship. Think about it. Inconsequential as it may be, when parents finally come clean about Santa Claus, the child's disappointment comes not from the fact that Santa doesn't exist, but rather from the realization that they have been deceived by the most important people in their life.

Each time we deny a child the factual understanding they instinctually thirst for, we incrementally hobble their innate efforts to succeed in life. All those seemingly trivial pieces of information they ask for are by no means trivial to them. They represent the elemental truths from which a child begins forming their picture of reality. And to the degree we fail to provide those truths or, worse yet, provide untruths, we deprive them of the tools they need to understand their experiences and develop a healthy relationship with reality.

CONSCIOUSLY GRASPING THE CONCEPT OF TRUTH

As straightforward and essential as truth is, none of us are born with an understanding of it. Because truth is not something we can see or touch, it takes several years before we're able to grasp the concept. Prior to that, we remain unaware of both truth and untruth, incapable of appreciating the real versus the unreal. We simply accept what we are told and take things to be as they overtly appear.

But in nature being naive presents risks, which is why we are such intellectual sponges when we're young. Our instinctual priority is to learn as much as we can as fast as we can, so that we can become self-reliant as soon as possible. This is why our desire for new experiences is so strong when we're young and wanes as we grow older. It is fueled by our instinctual drive for self-reliance.

Because truth and untruth only have meaning in the context of one another, we actually become aware of both simultaneously, instinctively recognizing them as tools that we can use. Our naïve accepting nature eventually gives way to a more realistic uncertainty, which in turn triggers the instinctual compulsion to question the validity and veracity of everything we experience. This is why children who are supported and encouraged tend to recognize reality better than those who are pressured and controlled. The process of learning to reason is instinctually driven, and while the former serves to facilitate that natural development, the latter acts to hamper and distort it.

WHAT DETERMINES OUR RELATIONSHIP WITH TRUTH

We learn virtually all the precepts we use throughout life subconsciously from our parents at an early age, our relationship with truth being among the most elemental and important. By the time we reach the age of about six or seven, not only have we developed the ability and acquired enough experiences to determine truth ourselves, we have become habituated in our desire to do so. Parents can either bestow upon their children the mental processes that embrace reality and foster success, or burden them with a lifetime of failed attempts to reconcile an increasingly distorted perspective.

Though the task of raising a child is extraordinarily difficult to perform well, the objective can be distilled to relatively few words. A parent needs to be truthful and encourage as many experiences as possible while preventing any permanent harm. The two factors that most enhance a child's intellectual growth are the extent of their experiences and the accuracy with which they interpret them. Because we learn from our experiences, the more we experience early in life, the more we're able to build upon that knowledge. The basic limitation being, our experiences only result in knowledge to the extent we accurately interpret them, hence the importance of helping our children learn to not deny the harsh realities that life so often presents, but rather to accept and deal with them in an objective manner. The more comfortable our children become with truth and reality early in life, the more likely it is they will lead happy, healthy, and productive lives, and pass the same on to their children.

TRUTH'S DEPENDENCE ON RATIONALITY

Only to the degree we remain rational can we discern truth and receive the benefits of doing so. Though we possess an innate need for both truth and comfort, they seldom entirely coexist, which means that we are constantly subconsciously choosing between them. It comes down to remaining rational and enduring the discomfort of a useful truth, or becoming irrational and denying that truth to escape its discomfort. And no matter how objective and truthful we perceive ourselves to be, we each form our own unconscious threshold at which we begin rejecting truth for the sake of our comfort. What's more, because our children unconsciously adopt our behavioral propensities, the ease and frequency with which we go from being rational to irrational often gets passed on to them.

Perhaps the most prominent manifestation of this early conditioning in rationality is our intelligence quotient (IQ). It's not just a coincidence that both our IQ and our degree of rationality are established early in life and remain relatively constant thereafter. Our IQ is but a measure of our ability to learn, which is determined by our ability to remain rational. Somewhat contrary to conventional thinking, the correlation that often exists between the IQs of a parent and child is not so much that of genetic inheritance, but rather that of early behavioral conditioning. This is why parents who are not mentally gifted can create a child that is. By filling the child's early years with objective learning experiences, parents don't just provide greater understanding when it can do the most good, they habituate the child in a more rational perspective.

The fact that, once established, our degree of rationality remains fairly constant is why people who listen poorly are likely to always do so. It's not that they don't hear what's being said. It's that we all unconsciously bend what we hear to concur with our picture of reality. The more irrational our thinking, the more distorted our picture, and the more we contort what we hear, to coincide with it. It's why people who are prone to making bad decisions generally continue to do so no matter how much anyone tries to help or explain things. Once our degree of rationality has formed, it largely determines our ability to reason. Hence the saying *you can lead a man to reason, but you can't make him think.*

And to the degree we become accustomed to irrational thinking it naturally gets reflected in our behaviors. Though we seldom construe our own behaviors as irrational, when the things we say or do lack reason, it becomes readily apparent to others. This is why an irrational person is rarely a happy person. To the extent we become habituated to the practice of relinquishing logic and reason, we lose our ability to communicate with others in any meaningful way, an affliction that parents have the opportunity to either curb or exacerbate in their children.

THE INSTINCTUAL PROCESS OF DETERMINING TRUTH

What makes human behavior so difficult to understand is that it includes a great many unconscious processes. Conscious thought makes it possible to understand almost anything. But, as strange as it sounds, it also impedes our understanding of human behavior. Precisely because we view things from a conscious perspective, we remain largely oblivious to all the natural processes that take place at the subconscious level. Trying to understand why we do things, without recognizing nature's unconscious input, is akin to guessing at a large jigsaw puzzle while looking at only a handful of its pieces. Worse yet, in the absence of such information, our natural tendency is not to simply accept the fact that we don't understand, but rather to create an entirely conscious explanation, effectively ensuring a false understanding.

Because all life must discern and react to that which is real, to survive, not only is truth a precious commodity throughout nature, but genetic instructions have come to determine it through unconscious processes. And because survival is ultimately a competition, all life is constantly vying to obtain truth. This is why many species have evolved to employ such purposeful deceptions as camouflage in their outward appearance. Whether predator or prey, it is often of benefit to conceal the truth of one's presence. The significance being, our desire for truth is not borne of conscious thought or moral stature, but rather of primal instinctual need. Just like every other animal, we instinctively perceive truth and reality regarding everything we experience, and naturally seek to use it to our own advantage.

To determine truth, just like with all our other instinctual processes, we utilize the information detected by our senses. It's how we learn anything and everything: we derive it from things that we know from our past experiences. This is why we must learn to count before we can add and add before we can multiply. We learn through a sequential process that builds upon itself, a process that effectively limits our new realizations to those most adjacent or related to our existing knowledge. Unbeknownst to the conscious mind, we are constantly comparing everything in our current experiences, regardless of nature or import, to everything we've experienced in the past, and instinctively perceiving what is true and real. This is why, even when it is of no consequence to our immediate circumstance, we are genetically instructed to store the information contained in our experiences. We later use that information at a subconscious level, to decipher new realities.

Because our highest instinctual priority is surviving the present moment, the subconscious process of perceiving truth takes place in real time. This is why whether we're conversing with a complete stranger or someone we know to be exceedingly honest and smart, if they say something that we know isn't true, we instantly recognize it. It's not that we are consciously choosing whom or what to scrutinize. It's that we are constantly subconsciously determining the validity and veracity of everything we experience, whether we consciously think we need to or not.

The fact that we determine truth instinctively at the subconscious level is why the vast majority of what we learn doesn't come from any classroom or lesson. Conscious instruction makes up but a tiny fraction of our learning experience, language being perhaps the best example. The predominant way we learn what words mean is not through conscious study or memorization, but by simply hearing them used; hence our ability to converse at such an early age. We unconsciously compare the context of words to all that we know and instinctively perceive their meaning.

DEVELOPMENT OF THIS UNCONSCIOUS CAPABILITY

As previously touched on, by the time we reach the age of about six or seven, our mental processes have developed enough and we've accumulated enough experiences to begin discerning truth and reality ourselves. This is why all children lose their beliefs in such fictional characters as Santa Claus at about this age. It's not that all older siblings decide to wait until then to pronounce such truths. Older siblings, because of their constant proximity, are just the most likely people to set those mental processes in motion as they become functional, and such fictional characters are just the low hanging fruit first to be realized.

When an older sibling informs a younger one that there is no Santa Claus, even though his or her motives may be less than magnanimous, it's generally a textbook example of how to educate. The term educate is derived from the Latin word educo, which means to educe, to draw out or develop from within. Teaching is but the practice of illuminating the specific things in someone else's experiences that, when pieced together, will cause them to arrive at a particular new realization. As the late 16th/early 17th-century Italian astronomer, physicist, and philosopher Galileo Galilei so eloquently put it, "You cannot teach a man anything; you can only help him to find it within himself."[3] To educate a younger sibling about Santa Claus, older siblings intuitively point to things that the younger child already knows, such as the fact that no one could visit every house in one night, or that many houses don't have a chimney for Santa to come down. It demonstrates that once we begin determining truth ourselves, we instinctively recognize how to help others do the same.

As we become teenagers and approach independent adulthood, we naturally begin to rely more on our own determinations. It's nature's way of preparing us for life on our own. This is why grownups around the world so often perceive teenagers as young know-it-alls. It's during this transitional time in our development that we begin voicing our own determinations, to test their validity and effectiveness. Unfortunately, as parents, we generally don't perceive it as budding adults stretching and testing their intellectual wings, but rather as an unattractive behavior of choice or influence, one that requires not understanding, guidance, and support, but discipline.

THE NATURAL EFFECTS OF DETERMINING TRUTH SUBCONSCIOUSLY

The fact that we perceive truth instinctively is why feelings such as confidence, certainty, trust, and respect cannot be given, willed, forced, or otherwise consciously created. Like all our other feelings, they are a direct physiological response to our instinctual perceptions, and therefore occur upstream of the conscious mind (i.e., our feelings are chemical changes that we become aware of only after they have materialized).

A common misperception is that we sometimes just accept what we are told. Because truth is essential to our survival, once we become capable of determining it ourselves, our genetic instructions ensure that we do. Other people often provide input, but that input is usually a tiny portion of the information our subconscious uses to make such determinations. No matter the subject or circumstance, how little we know or how much someone else knows, we naturally take all the information available to us, compare it to all our past experiences, and subconsciously determine its probable veracity. Even though most of us know very little about the medical field, whether we realize it or not, we never simply accept what the doctor tells us. Because we are always aware of such things as voice inflections, mannerisms, and general deportment, we listen to what the doctor says, observe how they say it, and subconsciously compare it to what we've seen and heard in the past, which is what prompts the desire for a second opinion.

The fact that all people instinctively reach their own final conclusions is the reason we find ourselves with such colorful phrases as "you can't fix stupid." No matter how flawed, a person will always instinctively decide things from their own perception of reality, which makes any habituation to irrationality a lifelong impairment.

THE BOUNDLESS POSSIBILITIES OF DETERMINING TRUTH OURSELVES

When others teach us, it makes learning easier. But that convenience comes at a price. The knowledge we receive from others is limited to what they know and contains the inherent influence of their perspective. For us to gain knowledge beyond that of our teachers and remain uninfluenced by their perceptions we must deduce it ourselves, an endeavor limited only by our desire and ability to process the vast information we have stored in our subconscious. It represents the most significant difference between such leading thinkers as theoretical physicist Albert Einstein and all the rest of us. Leading thinkers spend much more of their time deriving their own realizations, while the rest of us spend most of ours learning what others know. Though we each have an enormous amount of stored information at our disposal, because it is so much easier to have things explained to us, we spend relatively little time digging through it.

The additional effort it takes to draw from our experiences is perhaps the most notable difference in the mental processes of reading and writing. When we read, it's enjoyable because it enables us to easily replicate what the writer was thinking. We transform words into feelings through an unconscious process that occurs naturally. But in order to write, we must dig through our experiences to find and convert feelings into words, something that requires considerable conscious thought. This is why, while we can become immersed in a good book somewhat indefinitely, it's difficult to write well for more than a few hours at a time. The process of writing requires more effort.

Writing is more difficult than reading because it utilizes the same basic process by which we derive new realizations. While reading makes learning easier by sharing the realizations of others, writing develops the skills we need to access the boundless knowledge contained in the countless permutations of information we each have stored in our subconscious. Inconceivable as it may be from our conscious perspective, the answer to virtually any question can be found amongst the incalculable yet-to-be-connected pieces of information we each possess at the subconscious level. The more we read, the faster we learn. The more we write, the better we get at using that knowledge to derive entirely new realizations. Perhaps the day is nearing when we will encourage writing as much as we've encouraged reading, in an effort to transform every person into a prolific source of original knowledge.

2

The Limited and Limiting Role of Our Senses

Inherent in every religion is the assertion that human beings can gain knowledge of the supernatural. The obvious problem here is that our senses only detect physical phenomena, which means that a whole lot of people are deluding themselves with a false pretense of supernatural knowledge. This chapter speaks to the reality of our human limitations.

Our senses do not process information per se. Their role is limited to detecting the presence, nature, and extent of certain stimuli. Our senses gather information, which the brain then processes to determine our best response. The unheralded benefit of this limited role is that it causes us to take in and store the raw factual data that constitutes reality. We can and generally do subsequently distort that information. But should it ever become an instinctual priority, we always have what it takes to deal in reality.

Our senses are limiting in that they only detect physical stimuli and only a tiny fraction of that which exists. Our eyes detect certain wavelengths of light, our ears detect certain frequencies of sound, our nose and tongue detect certain chemical elements, and our nerve endings detect the presence of certain objects and energies, as well as their textures and temperatures, all of which are entirely physical phenomena. This is why of all the countless pieces of information that have ever gone from the unknown to the known, without exception, not a single one has ever been determined to be of a nonphysical nature or cause. Our awareness is by nature exclusively limited to physical things and events. There is no larger set of empirical data on the face of the Earth than that which demonstrates our absolute lack of knowledge regarding the supernatural. For anyone to embrace the supernatural as knowledge they must delude themselves enough to discount this gargantuan ubiquitous reality and reject all logic and reason.

The fact that most of us do not yet recognize our experiences as being entirely physical can be seen in how we use the word physical. We commonly misuse it in a limiting way, to exclude things of the mind and spirit. Because our thoughts and feelings are not tangible, we don't yet perceive them as being physical in nature and ultimately governed by the laws of chemistry and physics. But they are. This is how researchers are able to attach electrodes to the brains of quadriplegics and enable them to operate motorized wheelchairs and robotic appendages. They make use of the physical energies that are our thoughts and feelings.

The reason we still perceive certain aspects of the human experience as being nonphysical is partly out of a lack of understanding and partly out of emotional convenience. When we envision anything as being nonphysical, because we cannot deduce such things from our physical experiences, we must imagine them, a mental process that naturally lends itself to satisfying our emotional needs. Two good examples are the notions we commonly hold of a soul and spirituality. Because we still perceive them as nonphysical, we're able to embrace the rather comforting mystical notion that they survive death. But in reality, because we use these terms to represent the feelings that guide our behaviors and define who we are, no matter how each of us perceives them, we are talking about entirely physical phenomena governed by natural physiological processes within the body. This is why so many people are beginning to explore their spirituality independent of religion. We are becoming increasingly cognizant of the stark difference between the very real and beneficial nature of our spirituality and the imaginary and often harmful nature of religion.

3

How Information from Our Senses Becomes Our Behaviors

Because religion serves as an explanation for things we do not understand, the more we know about how our behaviors are produced naturally, the less need we feel to imagine such explanations. This chapter is dedicated to furthering that knowledge.

WE ARE A SPECIES OF ANIMAL

It is common knowledge that humans are classified as a species of animal. But virtually no one embraces all that that classification entails. When we see a behavior being exhibited in unrelated cultures around the world, it's safe to say that it somehow stems from our shared instinctual needs. But beyond such overt clues, the connection between our behaviors and our genetic makeup can be difficult to recognize, which leads to an overly simplistic understanding of why we do the things we do. Instead of recognizing how our behaviors are genetically generated, we simply see them as being consciously chosen, as if our conscious processes are somehow exempt from genetic instruction.

The fact that our mental capabilities have developed further than other species does not mean that we no longer rely on the underlying genetic processes by which all animals function. It just means that we have evolved to make them more efficient and effective. In the words of 18th-century political activist and author Thomas Paine, "He who takes nature for his guide is not easily beaten out of his argument."[4] Even though we don't always understand the things we do, from nature's perspective they are never without purpose. This is why necessity has been so aptly named the mother of invention. Instinctual need is the origin, impetus, and guidance for all behaviors. Thus, to understand any behavior we have but to decipher how it satisfies a need.

THE ESSENTIAL FUNCTION OF OUR EMOTIONS

While everyone realizes that we have feelings, we don't often recognize the natural cause and purpose behind them. Our feelings represent the physiological mechanism by which our genetic instructions prompt and steer everything we think, say, and do. As our senses detect things in the environment, our genetic instructions instantaneously determine whether they are potentially good for us or bad for us and trigger specific chemical changes that increase or decrease our level of comfort, to effectively encourage or discourage more of that experience. Accordingly, wherever I use the term *genetic response* in this text, I am referring to the chemical changes that our genetic instructions trigger upstream of the conscious mind (i.e., our emotions and feelings), to induce action, and not the action itself, which may or may not follow.

Our failure to recognize the function of our emotions is why we so often misattribute the behavior of lesser life forms to conscious thought. When an animal's behavior resembles what we might do in a similar situation, because we have yet to comprehend how unconscious processes produced that behavior, we naturally attribute it to the only processes we can fathom: conscious thought. In essence, we have it backwards. When an animal's behavior coincides with ours, it's not because they were consciously thinking the same things we were. It's because the same unconscious feelings that produced their behavior produced our thoughts. Conscious thought merely provides us the opportunity to refine the product of those feelings.

Because genetic instructions use how we feel to prompt and steer our behaviors, our first order of response is always unconscious and therefore irrational. Our behaviors, conscious or otherwise, are always preceded by a physiological chain reaction. Our senses detect stimuli in the environment and trigger chemical changes that alter the way we feel, all of which are physical events initiated by preceding physical events without the involvement of conscious thought. This is why it becomes more difficult to remain rational as our emotions intensify. Inducing action independent of thought is precisely the function of that physiological chain reaction. It's how even the simplest of organisms are able to navigate their environment to survive. Genetic instructions reduce the vast complexities of survival to simply doing that which feels best.

From our most subtle emotional comforts to our most intense physical pains, the things we feel at any given time are involuntary genetic responses to what we are experiencing at that time. The more instinctually important something is perceived to be, the more it contributes to what we feel and the less it facilitates conscious thought. This is why we so often have mixed feelings and, though our language is about five times more expansive than during Shakespeare's time, we still struggle to articulate the intricate nuances of how we feel. Largely unbeknownst to the conscious mind, our experiences produce a continuum of complex and ever-changing emotions.

The fact that our feelings serve specific instinctual needs can be seen in the differing emotions of men and women. It is through these genetically triggered chemical changes that nature differentiates the roles of male and female. Again, our feelings are not controlled by, but rather give rise to, the things we think, say, and do. This is why when making difficult decisions we often hear such advice as "Go with your gut instinct" or "Listen to your heart." Even though we don't yet grasp how our feelings are produced, we intuitively recognize and value the primal guidance they provide. As 19th-century British Prime Minister and author Benjamin Disraeli put it, "Never apologize for showing feeling. . . when you do so, you apologize for the truth."[5]

We can actually influence the things we feel, but only preemptively. Much like a computer, if we want our genetic instructions to produce a different feeling, we have only two choices. We can either modify the code that determines their output, or we can present them with different input. And though mood-altering medications might be considered a temporary change to our genetic program, at this point the only real control we have over our feelings is our ability to consciously choose the experiences that produce them.

Even when our actions are consciously determined, our thoughts have been prompted and guided by chemical changes intended to address our particular situation. When determining which flavor or color we like best, what we're actually doing is trying to discern the subtle differences in how they make us feel. Though we may not understand why our genetic instructions perceive such things differently, we instinctively follow their primal guidance to make our choice. Though we perceive it as a 'conscious choice,' we're actually just trying to realize a determination that has already been made at the subconscious level.

This basic understanding, that our feelings serve to induce action independent of thought, is crucial to improving human behavior. Whether it's a child trying to keep from being provoked, an adult trying to control their temper, or a law enforcement officer trying not to overreact when apprehending a suspect, it is the ability to remain rational that ultimately determines their success, an ability that can be greatly enhanced by a real time awareness of these instinctual promptings.

LIFE IS ALL ABOUT HOW WE FEEL

Because the things that cause us to feel good are by nature those things that have proven to provide benefit, we have but one instinctual objective, to feel as good as we can as much of the time as we can. The trick of course is to make decisions that cause us to feel the best not just in the here and now, but over time, which makes the perpetual challenge one of better recognizing the longer-term effects of our behaviors. It's why life is all about the journey and not the destination. Every thought we think and action we take is in some way an instinctual effort to improve how we feel, all of which occurs not at the end of life, but throughout the course of life.

A somewhat subtle aspect of our feelings is that, because they occur in real time, they are never a response to the past or the future. If we learned that a loved one had died several days earlier or was about to die, the immediate emotion we felt would be a genetic response not to the actual event, but to us experiencing that information in the present. This is why we possess a natural penchant for immediate gratification. Because their priority is to prompt actions that improve our immediate circumstance, our feelings are by nature nearsighted. They have evolved to reflect the basic fact that if we do not survive the present moment, the future is of no consequence. Hence the considerable benefits of a conscious awareness and the ability to selectively override them.

THE IRRESISTIBLE ALLURE OF OUR GENETIC GUIDANCE

As the 19th-century American showman Phineas Taylor Barnum, better known as P.T. Barnum, is often credited with saying "If you want to draw a crowd, start a fight,"[6] which he is said to have done when he wanted to hand out flyers for an upcoming event. The fact that our feelings provide instinctual guidance is why we are drawn to emotion. The more instinctually significant a circumstance, the more emotion we feel and the more it captivates our attention. This is how and why it is our emotions that make life so rich. They represent the instinctual value of the things we experience.

The inexorable pull of our emotions is what makes the ability to evoke them such an invaluable tool in the hands of anyone wanting to manipulate or control others. This is why so many of the news, history, and educational channels on television have now purposefully compromised their objective programming, to include subjective drama. They have come to realize that emotions ultimately trump intellect when it comes to garnering our attention.

Whether we're writing, speaking, or simply giving someone a look, what we're so often doing is trying to convey a feeling that will elicit the response we want. It's not that we dislike the other person or have some untoward plan to take advantage of them. It's that we always instinctively use everything at our disposal to our own advantage, and emotion is one of our most effective tools.

THE DISTORTING EFFECTS OF OUR GENETIC GUIDANCE

Because our genetic instructions leverage our comfort to shape our behaviors, our natural proclivity is not to be objective, but rather to think, say, and do whatever it takes to feel better. This is the essence of our subjective nature. To improve how we feel, we are constantly distorting our own perception of reality. Such is the intrinsic conundrum of conscious beings. We need our emotions to propel and guide us through life, yet we need an absence of emotion to understand it.

Despite their essential nature, because emotions hamper rational thought, they are, and always will be, the ultimate hindrance to learning and achieving. When anyone intentionally evokes emotion, it is necessarily not for the purpose of advancing awareness. To the contrary, because emotion induces action independent of thought, the more we feel, the more it dominates and hinders the rational processes needed to achieve understanding.

A rather stark example of emotionally driven distortion made headlines in 1995 when O.J. Simpson was acquitted of double murder. Shortly after the verdicts were announced, a CBS News poll[7] showed that 78% of the black respondents thought he was innocent, while 75% of the white respondents thought he was guilty. It wasn't that these two groups were exposed to different facts or that one was smarter than the other. It was that we each naturally distort our experiences in a way that caters to our emotional needs, needs that remain markedly different for each race.

This natural self-serving distortion in our perspective is why we need double-blind procedures in studies and experiments that involve human beings. No matter how impartial we try to be at the conscious level, we are powerless to preclude our personal biases from influencing our perspective at the subconscious level. It's fundamental to why men and women experience things differently. We each distort our perceptions to satisfy our emotional needs, needs that are by nature purposefully different for men and women.

OUR INNATE DISCOMFORT WITH THE UNKNOWN

Because unknowns can adversely affect our chances of survival, our genetic instructions have evolved to deal with them by making us uncomfortable in proportion to the risks they pose. This is why, though there are always things that we do not know, our level of discomfort is seldom perceptible. Only unknowns that are instinctually perceived as critical produce enough discomfort to reach the level we consciously recognize as fear.

The untold story of these instinctual promptings is that they don't always produce helpful behaviors. For the most part, the chemical changes that make us fearful do in fact serve their intended function. They prompt us to either acquire the missing knowledge or change our circumstances to no longer need it. But when neither action is possible, these same chemical changes often induce a rather nearsighted shortcut to comfort, in the form of an imagined explanation that we embrace as knowledge. This is how and why past generations came to imagine supernatural explanations for plagues, earthquakes, eclipses, and other significant natural events they didn't understand. Such self-created faux knowledge served as a kind of psychological workaround to ease the discomfort of not knowing. It's why an air of certainty about the hereafter is essential to the success of any religious leader. It enables them to ease the considerable discomfort of nature's most significant unknown in their audience, a duplicity for which there is high demand.

OUR DISPROPORTIONATE AVERSION TO DETRIMENT

If we were given the opportunity to win or lose one hundred dollars on the flip of a coin, most of us would decline the offer. We recognize that, even though the risk and reward are exactly equal, the feeling of losing a hundred dollars is discernibly greater than that of winning a hundred dollars. The basic instinctual reason behind this is that while positive things can enhance our survival, negative things can end it. This is why physical pain can be so much greater than any pleasurable feeling. Physical injury can have a greater, more immediate effect on our existence.

Our disproportionate discomfort with detriment is a large part of why political candidates more often slander their opponents than tout their own virtues and abilities. Evoking a fear of what their opponent might do is by nature more effective than stating what they them self would do. It's why we're considerably more likely to hear "You're going to hell" than "You're not going to heaven." Religious leaders have learned that they can exploit our innate propensity to err on the side of safety by preaching not the love of God but rather the fear of God.

4

Nature's Exceptionless Mandate That We Benefit Ourselves

Perhaps the most common misperception regarding religion is that it serves to shape our behaviors. This chapter explains how all our behaviors, the good and the bad, are naturally generated not by the things we consciously imagine, but rather by our genetic instructions interpreting the real things in our environment to effect our survival.

All life is hardwired to do one thing, act in its own best interest. The genetic directive to seek benefit is the most fundamental and universal in all of nature. It constitutes the sole function of our genetic instructions. For that reason, contrary to conventional thinking, the question is never *if* but rather *how* we should want to benefit ourselves. Because self-benefit is the sole all-inclusive impetus for our actions, in spite of how it may often seem, our actions are never random, accidental, or selfless. They may not always produce the desired result, and they may at times result in unintended effects. But whether it's something as basic as a sunflower following the sun across the sky, or something as complex as one human being saving the life of another, every action of every living thing is always for the purpose of enhancing its own survival. This is why the human spirit, our principal animating force, flourishes in an environment that offers opportunity; that's what triggers the primal genetic impulses that make us productive.

The genetic mandate to acquire benefit is why it feels good to be productively engaged in a project or endeavor. It's why we enjoy doing things well and why we naturally strive to make tomorrow better than today. Those positive feelings are how our genetic instructions encourage self-benefitting behaviors. This is why life is not about getting to a point where we can do nothing, but rather getting to a point where we can do what we want. No less than the ants that perpetually move sand, we are being continually impelled to improve our existence. It's the fundamental reason, whether it's our legal system, a sporting event, or simply a friendly debate, our social processes and activities are often adversarial in nature. Life is a competition and nature has scripted every living thing to look out for itself.

One of the earliest materializations of this genetic mandate can be seen in the differing personalities of siblings. On the surface, it might seem odd that children from the same family end up with radically different personalities. But it's not only natural; it's inevitable. Because life is a competition, and our early survival is dependent on the attention given us by adults, one of the first things we learn is how best to vie for that attention. We instinctively learn that by behaving differently we can garner more of our parents' focus, which over time develops into our own unique personality. This is why the first two children of any family tend to differ most. When the second child arrives, their innate desire to be different naturally results in behaviors somewhat opposite of the first, with subsequent children finding behaviors somewhere in between.

Our genetic mandate to acquire benefit is the fundamental reason, regardless of language, time in history, politics, religion, culture, geographic location, or natural resources, virtually any form of capitalism flourishes, while most forms of socialism struggle to survive. When we exchange goods or services, we gain access to benefits we could not otherwise attain. Economic systems such as capitalism and socialism are merely the organized rules and processes by which we make such exchanges. Ergo, the better they are at facilitating those exchanges, the more benefits they make possible. Capitalism is consistently more successful than socialism because it allows prices to reflect the actual value of goods and services as determined by scarcity and need, a paradigm that naturally encourages trade and commerce. Socialism, on the other hand, imposes artificial prices that conflict with actual values. Capitalism also allows exchanges to be made directly between the parties, making it easy to see which behaviors produce the greatest benefit. While socialism requires that people contribute to and draw from the government with little or no consideration given to the size of their contribution, a process that discounts the instinctual connection between effort and reward, significantly diminishing the impetus to work and produce. Capitalism is more successful than socialism because it is perceptibly more efficient and effective at facilitating the fundamental genetic objective of procuring benefit.

Genetic instructions have come to know how and where benefit can best be attained, through countless natural generational differences. Because nature combines the genes of two different organisms to create the next generation, each new generation is somewhat different than the previous. And no matter how slight those generational differences are, they impact each new organism's ability to attain benefit, sometimes for the better, sometimes for the worse. But no matter how random those new traits may be, their effect on the species is anything but. Offspring born with improved traits live longer than those born with diminished traits, resulting in beneficial qualities being reproduced more than diminished qualities. The natural result being, the species improves over time. The unconscious physiological mechanism that we call genetic instruction is continually improving life because even the happenstance of generational differences results in ever more beneficial traits and behaviors. Because genetic instructions contain not just the impetus that continually urges life to pursue benefit but also the cumulative history that delineates which behaviors provide benefit, they comprise both the animating force and the innate compass by which all life navigates its environment to effect its own survival.

OUR TWO BASIC AND MUTUALLY EXCLUSIVE TYPES OF BENEFIT

While it may be easy to see that our genetic instructions prompt us to pursue benefit, it's often difficult if not impossible to recognize the benefits our behaviors are intended to produce. The primary reason being, we are a species of social animal, which means that we seek two very different types of benefit. We do things that benefit ourselves directly as individuals, and we do things that benefit us indirectly by enabling us to become part of a group.

Since sharing risks and pooling resources significantly improve our chances of survival, our genetic instructions have evolved to encourage behaviors that facilitate living and working with others. It's what differentiates social animals from all other animals; they have evolved to exhibit behaviors that acquire benefit through coexistence. This is why it's somewhat disingenuous to take credit for helping others. Because all our behaviors are prompted and guided by genetic instruction, absolutely everything we think, say, and do is but a reflection of how we perceive we can most benefit ourselves.

Our instinctual impulsion to consider others is what enables our legal system to maintain that ignorance is no excuse for violating the law. It's not that every person can be expected to learn and remember the countless laws we create. It's that our laws merely delineate behaviors that are harmful to others, behaviors that go against our innate need for acceptance, which makes them intuitive to everyone. This instinctive thirst for acceptance is what makes social networking sites and "friending" so popular. It's also why, in spite of anyone's claim to the contrary, we do in fact care what others think about us. Whether it's our appearance, the things we say, or how we act, because we are instinctually impelled to do so, we always at least subconsciously consider how it will be received by others. This is why clowns make so many people uncomfortable. The visual effect created by a clown's makeup often precludes others from discerning what the clown is feeling toward them, which makes the experience instinctually disconcerting.

Our innate need for acceptance is why money is limited in its ability to make us happy. Though it can secure such tangible necessities as food, clothing, and shelter, money does nothing to improve who we are, which means it can only contribute superficially to satisfying this powerful instinctual need. Our considerable need for acceptance is why hate crimes are so incredibly harmful. When we are rejected because of our race or sexual orientation, and therefore powerless to do anything about it, we perceive it as an insurmountable obstacle to the acceptance we so desperately need, a perception that can have devastating psychological effects.

What's important to understand about the human need for acceptance is that the instinctual impulses that prompt it make no distinction regarding whom we should seek out to satisfy it. They merely speak to the fact that there is safety in numbers, that we can enhance our survival by forming alliances. What this effectively means is that, because these impulsions begin in earnest as we reach adolescence, we become susceptible to joining any group before we're able to apprehend the consequences of joining the wrong group. These natural impulsions are what enable gangs and cults to recruit young people who feel rejected by society. They satisfy this powerful instinctual need for acceptance when others can't or won't.

Because individual and group behaviors are exclusive of one another, we must constantly choose between them. They result in what psychologists have dubbed exchange and communal relationships[8]. Exchange relationships serve to facilitate a direct transfer of benefits, while communal relationships serve to facilitate the indirect benefits we receive by becoming part of a group. Researchers have also determined that two separate portions of the brain govern these two distinctly different types of behavior. Behaviors that benefit us directly are initiated by the nucleus accumbens, often referred to as the brain's pleasure center, while behaviors that benefit us through the group are initiated by the posterior superior temporal sulcus, often called the brain's altruism center. And consistent with these behaviors being mutually exclusive, researchers have found that these two areas of the brain do not function simultaneously, creating the physiological divide that causes us to choose between them.

The genetic directive to act in our own best interest naturally impels us to seek the greatest benefit, regardless of whether it comes from individual or group behaviors. The more adept we become at recognizing the often subtle, complex, and distant benefits of being part of a group, the more we naturally exhibit social behaviors. This is why some people are greedy while others are generous. It's not that they differ in motive, for all creatures are exclusively driven by the desire to benefit themselves. It's that no two people are equally adept at recognizing which behaviors provide the greatest benefit.

The fact that we derive the greatest overall benefit through a combination of individual and group behaviors is why, by nature, there is an optimum amount that we should pay in taxes. Regardless of what the pundits and politicians say, taxes are not about what segment of the population should pay more; they are about finding the optimum amount that should be taken from individuals and applied to the group, to produce the greatest overall benefit to society as a whole. The instinctual constraints being, the more we tax individuals, the less impetus they feel to work and produce. While the less we tax individuals, the fewer resources there are for communal benefits.

The fact that we choose between individual and communal behaviors based on which provides the greatest benefit is what makes equal taxation essential to a healthy society. When government fails to serve everyone, but instead takes money from some people and gives it to others, subtle as it may be, it sends the unconscious message that life is not about working together, but rather about getting what we can for ourselves. It fosters a kind of 'what's in it for me' mindset that naturally encourages more individual behaviors and fewer social behaviors, something that will eventually tatter the fabric of any society. Hence the essential need for our federal income tax to be a single flat rate with absolutely no deductions. When everyone is affected equally, it has a natural unifying effect, which in this case would be a significant force against wasteful spending.

If we want to increase social behaviors, we need to realize that seeking the greatest benefit is neither a good thing nor a bad thing, but rather a genetic thing. We need to understand that no matter how religious or righteous we perceive ourselves to be, when government makes individual behaviors the most attractive option, we will naturally abandon social behaviors to engage in them. Though its origin is uncertain, everyone understands the old adage "Give a man a fish and you feed him for a day; teach a man to fish and you feed him for a lifetime." What we don't seem to yet grasp is that learning how to provide for ourselves is not enough. We must also possess the innate desire to do so, an instinctual impetus solely produced by the prospect of benefit. If there is someone standing on the dock handing out fish, even the best fishermen will stay in port.

To understand our behaviors we must look beyond the notion of consciously choosing them, and recognize that they are always fueled by a natural unconscious desire to improve our existence. We must come to realize that our rules, laws, and systems exist exclusively for the purpose of facilitating our coexistence and that they will only succeed to the extent they facilitate that entirely natural objective. If the advantages of abiding by the rules are not perceived as offering more benefit than violating them, we will by nature act to benefit ourselves individually at the expense of the group.

OUR PERPETUAL DILEMMA OF TRUTH VS. ACCEPTANCE

Because the need for acceptance is a significant instinctual priority, it permeates every aspect of our lives. A great example is our desire for political correctness. Being politically correct is nothing more than artfully replacing that which is factually accurate with that which is more psychologically palatable, for the purpose of facilitating our acceptance. Political correctness represents the degree to which we are willing to compromise objective truth, to be accepted by others. The net effect is that we often placate our audience at the considerable expense of solving our problems, effectively trading a better tomorrow for a more comfortable today. Such is our human nature.

To receive the acceptance of others, we instinctively censor our thoughts and feelings before they become manifest in word or deed. This is why our true nature only surfaces in fleeting moments, generally amidst trying times. We subconsciously know that our raw thoughts and feelings reflect our innate self-interest the voicing of which must be tempered to sustain our acceptance. Inherent in the human experience is the perpetual dilemma of having to decide when and with whom to be forthright. This is why we so value those to whom we can speak frankly and openly. As the 19th-century author, poet, and philosopher Ralph Waldo Emerson so succinctly put it, "A friend is one before whom I may think aloud."[9] To afford someone the opportunity to speak their mind without concern for their acceptance is indeed a rare and treasured gift.

This powerful instinctual need creates a kind of hill that truth must traverse on its way to becoming common knowledge. Because it enhances our acceptance to adopt the group's perspective, we feel impelled to reject new truths until a majority embraces them. When the first few people realized and declared that the Sun did not revolve around the Earth, that it was actually the other way around, they were ridiculed and shunned, which had the effect of discouraging others from embracing their discovery. It's an effect that can be seen in today's political arena and its vacuum of leadership. Because popularity reigns supreme as their decision-making criteria, politicians rarely support initiatives until they have found favor with a majority.

THE SEDUCTIVE ILLUSION OF SELFLESSNESS

Because every action of every living thing is genetically initiated for the purpose of self-benefit, there is no such thing as a selfless act in nature. The term is but one of many oxymora that we have yet to recognize. Our desire to perceive and present ourselves as generous or selfless is but another manifestation of our need for acceptance. This is why we often mistakenly villainize money and/or capitalism. Money is just a convenient medium through which we exchange goods and services, and capitalism is just an efficient system for conducting such exchanges. They fall victim to negative connotations because we have yet to recognize that all of nature is exclusively driven by self-benefit. Money and capitalism are not bad, nor do they make us bad. They merely reflect the harsh reality of our innate self-interest. They are the unfortunate messengers that most often deliver the truth that we are not as selfless as we'd like to believe.

Contributing to our mistaken notion of selfless behavior is the fact that there isn't always someone present to appreciate our actions. Simple logic tells us that if social behaviors are to enhance our acceptance, someone must become aware of them. Yet it isn't all that difficult to find examples of people doing things that help others even when no one is around, a reality that would seem to support the notion of a selfless act. And that would indeed be valid reasoning if our behaviors were consciously initiated, but they are not. Again, all our behaviors are prompted and guided by genetic responses that are triggered at the subconscious level, which becomes apparent when we look at why we engage in such behaviors. We help others (even when no one is around) because it makes us feel good. It produces a positive feeling genetic response the natural purpose of which is to encourage social behaviors. Because such behaviors enhance our survival by not just elevating our acceptance, but also by strengthening the group, the genetic responses that prompt them have evolved to do so whether anyone is present or not.

THE NATURE BEHIND GOOD AND BAD BEHAVIORS

Without question, the most significant and widespread misconception regarding human behavior is that of religion improving it. The equation that determines how we behave was shaped by nature long before we acquired the ability to imagine any religion. Our genetic instructions have evolved to advance our survival by taking advantage of the repeatable effects found in the physical stimuli our senses detect (i.e., they utilize the recurring nature of physical cause and effect relationships). Because the nonphysical things we imagine produce no repeatable effects, they are of no consequence to the physiological processes that have evolved over millions of years to prompt and guide behaviors that enhance our survival. This is why around the world and throughout history religious people have not behaved better than the nonreligious. Because our species is that of a social animal, all people experience the instinctual urge to live amongst others, the natural force that impels good behavior.

All our behaviors, good and bad, are produced by the same genetic processes and instinctual needs, and are a reaction to the physical things we instinctually determine to be true and real. Good behaviors occur when we perceive that we will receive the greatest benefit by acting in support of the group. Bad behaviors occur when we perceive that the greatest benefit will come from acting to benefit ourselves at the expense of the group. This is the human nature side of crime and corruption, why we break the rules when we do. We are physiologically programmed to take the path that we perceive will produce the greatest benefit, hence the need for society to attach consequences to behaviors that harm the group. This is why if the entire world were to wake up one day with no awareness or recollection of religion, people would not suddenly begin engaging in reprehensible or immoral behaviors. The instinctual processes that have been determining our behaviors all along would still be performing their functions and resulting in the same proportion of good and bad behaviors. We would each remain the person we are, just without all the conflicts that invariably result from pretending that we have knowledge of the supernatural. The charitable work that is currently done in the name of religion would still be done, likely even more with all the additional money that the Church currently spends on promoting its holy righteous image. The lessons taught by religious fables and parables would still be taught, just without all the make-believe, in the much less harmful realm of truth and reality.

When we talk about individual behaviors versus group behaviors, the group ultimately consists of all mankind. But until we see ourselves as one large group, much like teenagers joining a local gang, we will naturally assimilate into and adopt the perspective of whatever local groups satisfy our need for acceptance. And because religious groups serve to ease some of our greatest discomforts, they will remain somewhat irresistible to a great many people. But because any religion comprises a group of people satisfying each other's need for acceptance, through a shared delusion of supernatural knowledge, that same dynamic serves to pressure support for whatever irrational behaviors emerge from that group. This is what gives religion the potential for massive harm. The expectations of the group, rational or not, become the baseline from which one's acceptance is determined. This is why social behaviors vary significantly around the world. They are governed by our need for acceptance, which makes them a product of each group's culture and awareness. As the 20th-century German psychologist and philosopher Erich Fromm wrote, "Once a doctrine, however irrational, has gained power in a society, millions of people will believe it rather than feel ostracized and isolated."[10]

The fact that good behaviors are caused not by religion, but rather by the instinctual need to coexist, is unequivocally demonstrated by every other species of social animal. Even though they lack the conscious capability to envision any kind of religion, honeybees spend their entire lives taking care of the queen. Because social animals are genetically directed to exhibit behaviors that facilitate coexistence, they all exhibit what we commonly think of as good or selfless behaviors. As far as such mythical forces as good and evil or God and the Devil, they are but imagined explanations we have consciously created to try and make sense of our behaviors.

WHEN OUR NEED FOR ACCEPTANCE BECOMES SECONDARY

Instinctually speaking, the need to live as part of a group provides so much benefit that it is exceeded only by the need to survive in the moment. Because our behaviors are governed by genetic instruction the sole purpose of which is to ensure our survival, when we feel threatened, at risk, or otherwise under duress, our behaviors become less about seeking the longer-term benefits of being accepted, and more about securing our well-being in the here and now. It's a reality borne out by rising crime rates during difficult economic times. As financial pressures increase, our scruples instinctively become subject to compromise. Our immediate needs begin to dominate over the longer-term benefits of finding favor with the group.

The fact that social behaviors are instinctually secondary to our immediate survival can also be seen in how we deal with terrorism. Profiling and torture are two good examples. Because a substantial majority of the terrorists to date have been of Middle Eastern descent, whether we consciously want to or not, and harmful as it may be to all the Middle Easterners who have no affiliation with terrorism, we unconsciously profile people who appear to be from that region of the world. We are instinctively impelled to pay more attention to individuals with physical traits similar to the people who have perpetrated such atrocities. Our conscious capabilities can help us to keep from overreacting to such impulsions. But to simply paint such feelings as wrong, without recognizing their natural origin and purpose, only makes them more difficult to understand and overcome when it's warranted. As it stands today, because outward appearance presents one of the biggest obstacles terrorists must overcome to accomplish their missions, it is as certain as our genetic mandate to survive that, no matter what we consciously think, we are not going to entirely remove that obstacle until we feel safe in doing so (i.e., profiling will exist whether we consciously like it or not). And the same applies to torture. Even though we consciously recognize that it's sometimes only marginally effective and can have considerable repercussions, the more threatened we feel, the more inclined we become to abandon our social concerns and engage in any behavior that might elevate our more immediate chances of survival.

The fact that our immediate safety takes precedence over social concerns is why as wars become more intense civilian casualties become somehow more tolerable. It reflects the basic reality that, by nature, our ability to show concern for the plight of others is somewhat proportional to and contingent upon us feeling safe and secure. A rather extreme example was the internment of more than 120,000 Japanese-Americans during World War II. Because Americans felt threatened, we took the extreme measure of imprisoning an entire race. And if you think that because we are more enlightened and civil now that it couldn't happen again, you are very much mistaken. Because such behaviors are instinctually driven and our genetic priorities haven't changed, such events are always as close as our next significant fear.

No matter how doable it may seem during times of peace, eliminating behaviors such as profiling and torture is and always will be an instinctual luxury afforded us only to the extent we do not feel threatened. This is why framing our debates on such subjects in terms of merely right or wrong hinders our efforts to diminish such unwanted behaviors. Until we recognize that the instinctual value of such behaviors is and always will be determined on a sliding scale of need and awareness, we will remain inept at dealing with them.

5

The Ever-Present Influence of Our Unconscious Associations

Religion denounces those who judge others. Yet, religious or not, we all do it. This chapter explains the natural reasons why and the paramount importance of this instinctive behavior.

A significant, though largely overlooked, influence on our behavior comes from the associations we instinctively make. Because truth is essential to survival, we have evolved to discern it regarding not just the present, but the future as well. Because anticipating what is about to occur has always held considerable benefit, long before we could consciously deduce such things nature developed an unconscious process to perform that function. Just like every other animal, our natural biological progressions have come to form a physiological link between the things we experience and the feelings that follow. By doing so, when we encounter those things a second time, we recall not just the previous encounter, but how it made us feel, which gives us a kind of unconscious heads-up on how it's likely to affect us.

The significance of linking our feelings to the things we experience is that those chemical changes embody our genetic assessment of how things impact our survival. By immediately recalling how something made us feel in the past, we're able to use our reactive genetic responses in a preemptive way, to predict how the things we encounter are likely to affect us. It's a process that enables life to learn from experiences without having to understand them. This is why animals with no conscious capabilities sometimes exhibit a strong fondness or aversion for specific people or things they've experienced in the past. It's not that they consciously deduce that such people or things are inherently good or bad for them. It's that they instinctively attach what they feel to whatever has their attention, and then naturally recall those feelings upon subsequent encounters.

These unconscious associations are why hearing a song from our past can change our mood. We recall not just the song, but many of the feelings we experienced when it was popular. It's why we like to keep photo albums. We enjoy recalling the feelings we have attached to the experiences they captured. It's how we're able to recall exactly where we were during significant events in history. The more emotion we feel, the stronger we attach it to the things we're experiencing at that time.

The bonds we form are but emotions we unconsciously attach to other living things. This is why soldiers who fought together often stay in touch even decades later. The strength of a bond is proportional to the emotion experienced. It's why the birth of a child is by nature one of the most emotional things we experience. The bond it produces is essential to the survival of the next generation. This is how and why an adult of one species will occasionally raise the offspring of another. Even though they share no genetic ties, the instincts in each trigger strong enough chemical changes to form a parent/offspring bond that dominates their behavior from that point forward.

Compared to our conscious processes, however, unconscious associations are not all that precise or effectual at foretelling future events. Because they merely link what we're feeling to the most prominent things we're experiencing at the time, unconscious associations represent nature's kind of shotgun approach to linking an effect to its cause. Sometimes they're correct and useful, and other times not. But since they produce a net benefit, (i.e., they produce more benefit when they're right than they incur detriment when they're wrong) genetic instructions have come to include them. When we link things that have no causal relationship, we often react in anticipation of events that are not likely to occur. But from nature's perspective, it's better to react too often and be safe than not to react at all and be sorry. A good example is when we find ourselves with an aversion to a particular food because it once made us sick. Even if we know that it wasn't the food itself but rather unsanitary preparation that caused the illness, because we have instinctively associated the feeling of sickness with the smell, taste, and sight of that particular food, when we experience any of those stimuli again, we recall how we felt and irrationally avoid it.

Crude as they may seem from our now conscious perspective, on an evolutionary scale it wasn't that long ago when these unconscious associations were the only means we had of anticipating our environment. Again, unconscious associations are how life evolved to learn without conscious thought, by taking advantage of the recurring cause and effect relationships in nature. The fact that human awareness has evolved to a conscious level in no way eliminates or precludes this or any other instinctual process from exerting influence on our behaviors. It just means that we have developed a more accurate method of processing the information our senses detect.

We've learned to use these unconscious links in many creative ways. Products are often displayed with an attractive model and/or popular music because, even though there is no functional connection, people unconsciously associate what they're feeling, with the product, and become more likely to buy. We've also learned that by artificially introducing an unpleasant feeling, such as nausea, simultaneous to an unwanted behavior, such as smoking, the patient associates the two and becomes less likely to repeat the behavior.

The fact that we still rely on unconscious associations to anticipate our environment can perhaps best be seen in situations where we have nothing else to go on, such as when encountering a complete stranger. Whether we realize it or not, we instinctively do everything we can to anticipate how people are likely to affect us, just as we do with everything else we encounter. Knowing nothing about their personality or character doesn't prevent our instinctual processes from making such assessments. It just limits the nature and extent of the information they have to work with. From an instinctual perspective, because even vague or incomplete information has value, we use how the stranger looks, their mannerisms, how they sound, and perhaps even how they smell, to determine how they are likely to behave. This is the elemental reason appearances matter. In the absence of more specific and substantive information, we instinctively rely on how such superficial attributes make us feel, to determine our behaviors. This is why we select the particular clothes, hairstyles, piercings, tattoos, and personal accessories we do. We intuitively recognize that it is our human nature to initially judge people by their outward appearance, so we take care in crafting our own.

The notion that we shouldn't judge others is, in a literal sense, little more than wishful thinking, for we are genetically programmed to do just that. It's the natural component that makes racism so enduring. No matter how repulsed we may be by the thought of it, we will instinctively associate skin color with behavior as long as there are perceptible differences in how the races behave. And for anyone who might think that no such differences exist, again, O.J. Simpson's acquittal in 1995 produced some rather stark and indisputable examples. While whites were largely shocked and saddened, blacks were largely jubilant and cheering. The relevance being, regardless of how such widespread behavioral differences came to exist, as long as they are perceptible, it gives instinctual cause to associate skin color with behavior, a natural subconscious generator of racism.

We like to view racism as a conscious malady, something that can be corrected through education and laws. But the truth is that a great deal of today's racism emanates not from ignorance, but rather from our instinctual recognition of legitimate behavioral differences, an uncomfortable reality that is seldom recognized and virtually never discussed. This is why our conscious efforts to eliminate racism produce ever-diminishing results. The conscious generators of racism, the ones that are easiest to deal with, are becoming an ever-smaller portion of the equation.

By nature, not until the races become indistinguishable in their behaviors will they instinctively perceive and treat each other as equals. Regardless of who or what the pundits blame, there are no simple fixes that can or will eliminate racism, and yielding to political correctness only delays the awareness that will eventually do the job. Difficult as it may be, when we are offended by what someone says, instead of having the kneejerk reaction of demanding that it not be said, we need to first ask if the comments are truthful. If they are, we should not just permit them; we should encourage them. By bringing our discomforting truths out for healthy scrutiny, we give them the platform they need to grow our common awareness.

6

Our Incredibly Useful and Occasionally Lethal Imagination

Because our senses are only capable of detecting physical phenomena, we are by nature precluded from becoming aware of anything supernatural, a fundamental reality that necessitates religion be entirely imagined. This chapter is critical in that it explains not just the process of imagining, but how and why it so often results in harmful behaviors when it comes to religion.

Thought can be separated into two basic categories: deductive reasoning, which deals with objective reality, and imagining, which deals with subjectively envisioning things we have not experienced. We're either trying to figure out and work with that which is true and real, or we're fabricating mental images of things that are not. And because both these processes are, like every other bodily function, driven by instinctual need, they result in a positive feeling when they accomplish their task. This is why it feels good to figure things out or envision things that, if realized, could satisfy a need. Those are the functions of deductive reasoning and imagining, respectively.

The fundamental difference between these two processes is that, unlike deductive reasoning, our imagination is not bound by the constraints of truth or reality. It is free to create whatever fanciful visions most improve how we feel. Hence our fascination with conspiracy theories, UFO's, Bigfoot, the Loch Ness monster, ghosts, and, yes, our notions of a God. Just like when we were little and found notions of unicorns, Santa Claus, and the tooth fairy fascinating and comforting, we still enjoy imagining mystical things that reach beyond truth and knowledge. We don't lose our desire to embrace what we imagine, as real. It just becomes more elaborate to remain plausible in the face of our growing awareness. No matter how illogical or nonsensical an explanation may be, if it caters to a strong enough need, we will embrace it as real in spite of all history, science, and reason.

Imagination is why the book is so often better than the movie. Because a book forces us to create our own visual images, our imagination naturally shapes them to best satisfy our specific emotional needs. While a movie, because it provides the visual images, is the psychological equivalent of one-size-fits-all. This is why partial nudity is more seductive than complete nudity. Anything left to the imagination is naturally filled in with that which best satisfies our needs. It's precisely what makes supernatural explanations so appealing, and oftentimes so harmful. When we're not able to understand our physical experiences, our imagination creates things that cater to our emotional needs. The all too often result being a nonphysical explanation that enhances our comfort at the expense of objective reality.

Though it's not something we often think about, the human experience comprises exclusively physical things and events, which means that even our imagination is limited to physical creations. This is why when we try to envision the nonphysical we necessarily end up with nothing more than an unrealistic picture of the physical. Since our imagination only has physical elements with which to work, all it can do is rearrange them in ways that we have not experienced. While certainly creative, the process of imagining is actually one of combining bits and pieces of that which is real, to form an image of something that is not.

The basic problem with embracing any type of nonphysical explanation is that it doesn't advance our understanding of the physical world in which we live; it hinders it. Because our knowledge is limited to the physical, and all the knowledge we have indicates that there is a physical explanation for everything we experience, if something nonphysical does exist, it is, for all intents and purposes, irrelevant to our existence.

Because we have not the slightest iota of information regarding the supernatural, the probability of us accurately guessing anything about it can be mathematically expressed as equaling one divided by infinity ($1/\infty$), a single blind stab into limitless possibilities, effectively nil. This is why our nonphysical explanations always conflict with reality. It's not that the nonphysical does not exist, for we have no way of knowing whether it does or doesn't. It's that we have absolutely nothing to guide us in constructing such explanations. All we have is our imagination, which is not just subjectively guided by how we feel; it is entirely limited to our physical experiences. Nonetheless, we routinely imagine nonphysical explanations and embrace them as knowledge, to ease the discomfort of not knowing.

If we are to purposefully advance in any way, the task before us is always one of understanding the physical. To help grasp the categorical difference between the natural and the supernatural, envision an infinite virtual plane separating everything physical from everything nonphysical. By definition, all science is deduced on the physical side of that plane and all religion is imagined on the other. As much as we might want to believe otherwise, science and religion share no common ground. All the people, things, places, and events described in religious texts are either real or imagined, and therefore necessarily exist on one side of that plane or the other, not both. Our efforts to combine them are but futile attempts to experience both truth and comfort where they are exclusive of one another. The significance of the supernatural does not lie in whether or not it exists or how it might affect us, but rather in how we deal with our complete absence of knowledge regarding it.

Another significant aspect of imagination is that it only enhances our comfort to the extent we convince ourselves that its creations are real or can be realized. This is how and why young children can more easily become captivated by fictional characters. Their limited grasp of reality enables them to more readily embrace their imaginings as real. It's also what makes that same self-deception potentially lethal when done by adults.

Because our genetic instructions encourage behaviors that provide benefit, we possess a natural propensity to imagine things that could make life better, independent of whether they can be realized or not. This is how we use imagination to design things that are useful. We envision things that make us feel good and then fold in logic and reason, to rationally determine how we might create them. By giving our ideas a virtual form, imagination makes us aware of yet unrealized ways of obtaining benefit, some feasible, some not. But to the degree we learn to utilize it as a tool, imagination opens the door to limitless possibilities. As Albert Einstein once stated, "A society's competitive advantage will come not from how well its schools teach the multiplication and periodic tables, but from how well they stimulate imagination and creativity."[11]

We've also learned to use imagination to create popular subjective designs. Though our imagination works to satisfy our own specific needs, because our basic instinctual needs are common to everyone, when we imagine something that makes us feel good, it quite often makes others feel good as well. We may not understand what need such creations fulfill, but to the degree we recognize how they make us feel, we can often create things that do the same for others.

When it comes to the things we imagine, we often overlook the fact that popularity does not determine reality. When many people imagine something similar or feel good about the same basic notion, it doesn't mean that they have envisioned something real. It just means that if that thing could be realized, it would satisfy a need that is common to many people. This is how and why we share so many of our misconceptions. When an unknown is common to many, the popularity of an imagined explanation is often misperceived as confirmation of its validity. In reality, as the late 19th/early 20th-century French writer Anatole France put it, "If 50 million people say a foolish thing, it is still a foolish thing."[12] When we arrive at something that is true or real, it is with all certainty not our imagination, but rather deductive reasoning, that has delivered us there.

7

Our Comforting Misperceptions of Conscious Choice and Free Will

Because religion serves as perhaps our most common explanation for things we do not understand, the more we know about how our decisions occur naturally, the less need we feel to evoke such imagined explanations as divine guidance. This chapter is dedicated to furthering that knowledge.

Our current perceptions of conscious choice and free will are among the most flawed notions we hold regarding human behavior. While we like to think of them as the unfettered ability to arbitrarily choose our actions, human nature speaks loudly to the contrary. Because we see things through the lens of a conscious being, we somewhat naturally embrace the conscious influences on our behavior, as being the only influences. This is how we arrive at such comforting notions as complete conscious control over our destiny. We are somewhat oblivious to all the unconscious input that goes into determining our behaviors, making our concepts of conscious choice and free will largely illusions of psychological convenience.

If we hear a three-year-old utter profanity, we naturally blame the parents and not the child. We recognize that the child's behavior is but a product of his or her environment. If we hear a twelve-year-old spew the hateful rhetoric of the extremist group in which they were raised, we also recognize it as the result of being brought up in such an environment. But because they are a little older, we find it a bit more difficult to hold them entirely blameless. And by the time a person reaches adulthood, because their conscious capabilities are fully developed, we hold them entirely responsible for the things they say and do. The fact that we get better at consciously controlling our behaviors as we age is why our legal system distinguishes between juveniles and adults. But the truth is, no matter how long we live, we never gain complete conscious control over our actions. We just move ever closer to it.

Because we instinctively learn from our experiences, and our genetic responses not just reflect what we've learned but are triggered upstream of the conscious mind, our past experiences always have an unconscious say in how we behave. The more impactful our early experiences, the more they influence subsequent behaviors, thus the fly in the ointment of conscious choice and free will. This is the underlying reason people so readily identify with such idioms as "they're cut from the same cloth" or "the apple doesn't fall far from the tree." We intuitively recognize that the experience of growing up with family influences all our behaviors thereafter. We're just not all that anxious to acknowledge such a shortfall in our own conscious control.

Because subconscious processes play such a large role in determining our behaviors, when we fail to recognize them it leaves a considerable void in our understanding, a void that we often fill with consciously imagined explanations. This is why complete understanding is necessarily exclusive of credit and blame. It precludes any need to fill in the blanks. To the degree we recognize that our behaviors are never the product of arbitrary choice, but rather always a natural attempt to attain benefit, our desire is not to credit or blame, but rather to understand the benefits they produce. It's why understanding and humility are inextricably entwined. Once we understand that our behaviors are a natural result, we no longer feel the need to take credit for them.

To understand how behaviors can be prompted and guided without consciously choosing them, envision a robot that has been programmed to play chess. It's an inanimate object containing a predetermined set of physical instructions that enable it to determine which actions are in its own best interest. Now envision that the robot has been programmed to learn from its experiences, and you get an idea of how our physical genetic instructions can result in behaviors even without conscious input. From our conscious perspective, we do effectively choose our actions, but because the process is much more instinctual and unconscious than we currently recognize, our choices are much more like the robot's than we like to think.

The role of the conscious mind is more often than not one of realizing decisions that have already been made at the subconscious level. Researchers have found that, even though we think of voluntary movement as being consciously determined, the signal to move a muscle actually occurs before we know we decided to move it.[13] In other words, when we think we are consciously choosing a behavior, we're actually just becoming aware of a behavior that has already been instinctually initiated.

Eventually, we will come to recognize that the absence of complete conscious control is nothing to be feared and that we have always lived with it. But until then, we will discount nature and overly embrace the comforting illusion of having it.

8

The Role of Conscious Thought in Determining Our Behaviors

Because religions reflect our limited understanding of the human experience, they somewhat naturally refer to human behavior as though it were exclusively determined by the conscious mind. But, as previously outlined, conscious thought is not the be-all and end-all of behavioral influences. There are millions of species of life on Earth and all of their behaviors, conscious or otherwise, are prompted and guided by genetic instruction. Even though it increasingly enables us to act in contrast to how we feel, conscious thought cannot and does not replace those feelings and the guidance they provide. It serves to refine the information our genetic instructions have to work with when determining our behaviors, a kind of beneficial app that we instinctively run if and to the extent circumstances allow. Accordingly, this chapter provides a basic understanding of that increasingly beneficial function.

THE SPAWNING OF CONSCIOUS THOUGHT

The reason we have difficulty grasping the role of conscious thought in our behaviors is that we seldom recognize it as a product of genetic instruction. We still think of our conscious processes as being independent and exempt from such physiological directives, when in fact they are neither. Once our genetic instructions determine that we need to act they still trigger the same preconscious chemical changes that begin urging us to act. It's just that now those chemical changes also prompt conscious thought. This is how genetic instructions give cause and direction to our conscious processes, and thereby refine their guidance. To the degree our circumstances afford us enough time, we incorporate our conscious determinations and our behaviors become more efficient and effective.

Our thoughts are not just subject to how we feel; they are subservient to our instinctual needs. And because they are guided by subtle changes in our level of comfort, their most elemental objective is by nature not to discern truth or reality, but rather to improve how we feel, hence our affinity for self-delusion. It's something that can perhaps best be seen in how we rationalize owning a gun. By far, the most common reason given for buying a gun is protection, to keep ourselves and our loved ones safe. But objective reality clearly demonstrates that buying a gun has quite the opposite effect.

Most gun statistics can be readily manipulated to support either side of the debate about owning them. There is one set of data, however, that remains immune to such purposeful distortions. It is the number and criminal status of people killed by private legally owned guns. When someone is killed by a legally owned gun, whether the victim is a criminal or just an innocent bystander, it invariably gets reported. And unlike lesser forms of gun violence where circumstances and outcomes can be, and virtually always are, exaggerated or misinterpreted, death is not a subjective state of being, making this data among the most accurate, complete, and reliable regarding the effects of owning a gun.

Federal Bureau of Investigation statistics show that, while they average killing less than 240 criminals nationwide[14], privately owned guns result in more than 21,600 suicides and unintentional deaths[15], every year. The simple indisputable reality being, a legally owned gun is at least 90 times more likely to end up killing an innocent person, than a criminal. And that doesn't include the thousands of homicides that are committed each year with guns stolen out of homes and vehicles, making the actual ratio much higher. If we were in a war and being annihilated by the enemy at the rate of more than 90-to-1, we wouldn't even think about rushing into battle. Yet, because our thoughts are prompted and guided by how we feel, we often create rationalizations that ignore such realities, and become 90 times more likely to destroy everything we hold dear, than to save it.

In effect, we have evolved to possess two distinctly different ways of arriving at behavior. On the one hand, we still have the same primitive impulsions that were once the only things determining our behaviors. Their predominant purpose and priority is to provide an immediate response to the things we encounter. And though the guidance they provide is relatively general, they excel in removing us from danger, with or without any conscious understanding of it. On the other hand, we now also have conscious thought, a mental process that enables us to not just assess situations with ever-greater depth and specificity, but to weigh the longer-term effects of many behaviors before choosing one. The former excels at removing us from immediate danger, while the latter excels at recognizing and procuring the greatest overall benefits.

THE IRRATIONAL PUSH OF OUR EMOTIONS TO SKIP CONSCIOUS THOUGHT

The fact that conscious thought and instinctual impulsions provide very different types of benefit is why what we *think* we should do so often differs from what we *feel* we should do. Our thoughts must effectively compete with our emotions to determine our behaviors. Paradoxical as it may be, the same preconscious chemical changes that prompt our behaviors somewhat impede the conscious input that can significantly improve them. A couple of ubiquitous examples can be seen in the behaviors of diet and exercise. Though we've learned that they provide greater benefits over time, diet and exercise remain difficult because they require us to consciously override our body's more immediate impulsions to store food and conserve energy. This is why we so often refer to a person as being weak or strong based on their ability to resist temptation. That temptation always comprises our instinctual impulsions. It's also why when we take the wrong action we usually err on the side of immediate gratification. Those impulsions are by nature predominantly focused on the here and now.

Perhaps the most notable example of the conscious mind being dominated by instinctual promptings occurs when we fall in love. Everyone knows that emotion diminishes our ability to think and act rationally, and that falling in love is arguably the ultimate example. We also know that choosing a lifelong partner is one of our most important decisions. So why is it that we are all so keen on having our judgment impaired when making such a lifelong commitment? The short and simple answer is that it feels so good. It exemplifies how our instinctual guidance, and not conscious input, has the ultimate say in determining our behaviors. This is why when looking back on our relationships we so often find ourselves pondering the rhetorical question *what was I thinking?!* The reality being, of course, that because of these powerful instinctual impulsions, there probably wasn't much thinking involved.

Our emotions impede understanding by overpowering the rational processes needed to achieve it. It's an effect that can be easily seen when dealing with inflammatory subjects, such as racism.

For instance, no word in and of itself should make us irrational, not even the N-word. It should always be the intent behind it (i.e., how the word is used) that determines our response. But that's something we invariably lose sight of when our emotions take charge.

Another instance of our emotions dominating over rational thought can be seen in the phenomenon known as mob mentality. Normally, we must choose between behaviors that satisfy our immediate impulsions and those that facilitate our acceptance. But when the group accepts irrational behavior, it effectively does away with the need to choose. Our two normally opposing behavioral influences become confluent, creating a single inordinately powerful urge to simply do what we feel without concern for our acceptance.

Mob mentality affords us but a brief glimpse into how incredibly important and powerful our instinctual need for acceptance is in determining our behaviors. Again, it is the sole driving force behind all social behaviors. This is what gives religion the potential for such incredible harm. When a number of people experience the same or similar feelings, that alignment of emotions can result in a sort of mutually accepted irrational norm that embraces harmful behaviors on the largest of scales.

But perhaps the most common example of our instinctual impulsions exerting an irrational influence can be seen in the disconcerting effects of our sexuality. Because we live amongst others, we are always expected to be accountable for our actions. But when we don't understand the feelings that prompt our behaviors, we find ourselves at a loss to explain them. Though they may be entirely natural and appropriate from an instinctual perspective, the things that stimulate us sexually are often inexplicable to the conscious mind. This is the essence of why we are ill at ease with our sexuality. We are prompted by unexplainable impulsions that subliminally encroach upon and menace our precarious notion of conscious control. The harm being, we often fabricate explanations that reach beyond truth and reality, to explain them.

Virtually all our internal conflicts are in some way a struggle to reconcile our instinctual urgings, with our conscious awareness. And the degree to which we fail gets reflected in our behaviors as a kind of irrational dysfunction. In the 1950s Elvis Presley's gyrating hips got him censored on television from the waist down. Fortunately, as we become more aware, we grow more comfortable with our sexual feelings, which means that at some point even today's behaviors will seem unnecessarily restrictive and perhaps silly. As strange and perhaps awkward as it may sound from our current perspective, alongside the birthing barn at your local county fair there may one day soon be a mating barn that will show this entirely natural part of the life cycle. Generally speaking, children don't have a problem learning nature's realities. We grownups have a problem dealing with how they make us feel. In other words, people don't end up needing therapy because they witnessed animals having sex when they were young. They end up needing therapy because of how their parents reacted to such events.

Our limited ability to make sense of these strong instinctual urges resides at the heart of virtually every social malady and psychological dysfunction having to do with our sexuality. It's why some people get upset about the sexual behaviors of complete strangers. It's not that they possess any special insight on morality or are exceedingly concerned about the wellbeing of people they don't know; it's that the thought of the behavior makes them uncomfortable. This is why some people look upon certain sexual acts as immoral, while others do not. It's the only way they know to make sense of what they feel. When a sexual behavior makes us uncomfortable but causes no harm, we find ourselves with no rational explanation for why we feel averse to it. The all too common result being, we come up with our own condemning explanations, to lend credence to those feelings.

This lack of understanding regarding our sexual feelings is why those who practice religion find themselves pressured to condemn homosexuality. Because people understood considerably less about their instinctual impulsions back when our many religious texts were being written, it was a certainty that homosexuality would be denounced as bad or wrong. What that means for anyone wanting to embrace those texts today, however, is that they must deny themselves the fundamental reality that our sexual feelings are instinctually triggered. Because these texts are supposed to reflect the word of God, as absolute knowledge, anyone wanting to follow them must delude themselves into thinking that one's sexual orientation is consciously chosen and can be changed at will. Even though they know that they themselves arrived at their own sexual orientation without making any such choice and that other species lacking any conscious capabilities exhibit homosexual behaviors, to embrace their religion they must distort their perspective enough to deny these realities.

The truth is that, while some would single out homosexual behaviors as capable of transmitting disease, not only can any form of sex spread disease when proper care isn't taken, but many heterosexual couples engage in the exact same behaviors. And while some would say that homosexuality is unnatural because it produces no offspring, it exists throughout the animal kingdom and perhaps always has. But such specious arguments persist because they serve to explain feelings we do not understand.

One of the most notable examples of such an alternative behavior being painted as bad or harmful took place in December of 2012, at Princeton University. As reported by the Associated

Press[16], while giving a talk there, the late U.S. Supreme Court Justice Antonin Scalia was asked by a gay student why he equated laws banning sodomy with those barring bestiality and murder. Scalia told the student "I don't think it's necessary, but I think it's effective." Scalia added that legislative bodies can ban what they believe to be immoral. "It's a form of argument that I thought you would have known, which is called the 'reduction to the absurd,'" said Scalia. "If we cannot have moral feelings against homosexuality, can we have it against murder? Can we have it against other things?" He then added, "I'm surprised you aren't persuaded."

For those who are not familiar with the term *reduction to the absurd*, it's merely a form of argument that seeks to demonstrate that a statement is true by showing that an absurd result occurs from its denial. The problem in this case, however, is that no such absurd result occurs. If the behavior Justice Scalia was referring to harmed others, like murder, then it would be absurd to think that we wouldn't have moral feelings against it, like we do against murder. But in fact, no such correlation exists, which is why the student and so many others were not persuaded by this argument, even when presented by a Supreme Court Justice.

The fact that Justice Scalia perceived such a correlation indicates that he was unable to distinguish between the behavior making him uncomfortable and it causing actual harm to society. It speaks to the essence of how and why our country is divided on the subject of homosexuality. We either see it as being harmful to society or as an innocuous relationship between consenting adults, with each perspective being somewhat incapable of comprehending how the other is not persuaded by what seems so obvious. Justice Scalia equated the morality of homosexual behavior to that of murder because in his mind they were somehow equally harmful to society. While the student and many others, both gay and straight, were able to recognize that, no matter how it makes us feel, there is no empirical data or evidence to support or even suggest such a correlation.

So how is it that a mere freshman in college was able to recognize this reality when a learned and illustrious Supreme Court Justice could not? Again, it comes down to the capacity of our feelings to influence our perception of reality. To the degree that homosexuality makes us uncomfortable, we are more likely to embrace explanations that portray it as wrong or harmful, to justify those feelings. But we're only able to recognize that reality if we do not feel an internal need to deny it, for our emotional needs are somewhat impervious to education and knowledge. Though Justice Scalia was well-versed in how to make his argument, his feelings kept him from recognizing the facts of what he was arguing. The basic lesson here is that no one is exempt from having their perspective distorted by what they feel and then having to imagine conscious explanations to rationalize it: hence the immense popularity of religion.

9

Nature in Our Relationships

IT'S ALL ABOUT THE BENEFITS WE RECEIVE

Because nature's sole objective is survival, we instinctively value things, both animate and inanimate, in proportion to how much they can benefit us, which in the case of living things is a function of their awareness. This is the underlying reason we value mammals more than insects and humans most of all. It's the nature behind theoretical physicist Stephen Hawking's concern that making contact with an alien life form could prove detrimental to mankind. Assuming that such aliens were more intelligent than humans and that they had evolved with the same intrinsic objective of survival, they would naturally treat us not as equals, but rather as lesser aware creatures, perhaps like we treat mammals or, even worse, insects.

Because all behaviors are ultimately an attempt to procure benefit, human relationships are but an implied understanding through which two people satisfy each other's instinctual needs. They represent nature's most essential form of reciprocity, a dynamic process of unconscious bartering the goods of which are the abilities and attributes that each person possesses. This is what makes the ability to listen such an attractive quality; it is essential to understanding our needs. It's also what makes every relationship so unique. We each have unique qualities to offer and their value is determined by someone else's unique needs. Hence the ageless saying "beauty is in the eye of the beholder." It's why we find it attractive when someone finds us attractive, and why we find it stimulating when we're able to stimulate someone else. Such things signify that we have an attribute or ability the other person desires, which means a relationship that could benefit us is possible.

The fact that relationships are all about acquiring benefit is why we find youth, beauty, strength, confidence, wealth, power, intelligence and even a simple smile attractive. They represent health, security, awareness, and acceptance, all things that are instinctually perceived to benefit ourselves and our offspring. This is why we sometimes fall in love at first sight. Many of the traits that are perceived to provide benefit are visibly apparent. It's why our expectations, both conscious and unconscious, play such a large role in determining the success of our relationships. To the degree two people share a common vision of the future, they are more likely to continue benefitting each other.

OUR QUALITIES AND TRAITS HAVE A MARKET VALUE

Because we always instinctively seek the greatest benefit, we naturally seek the most for what we have to offer in our relationships. This is why it's so fundamentally important to emphasize truth and bolster a child's self-esteem early and often. It is their perception of themselves, specifically their self-worth, which subconsciously determines the quality of the people they will seek out and accept in their relationships. If they perceive little value in what they have to offer, they will instinctively expect and settle for less in their relationships. Accordingly, the single most significant thing we can do to secure a good relationship is not to *find* a really good person, but rather to aspire to *be* a really good person. No matter how good a person we find, nature effectively ensures that we cannot sustain a relationship with anyone who has appreciably more to offer than we do. In short, you don't want to be looking for a partner and find yourself thinking *but who would want to be with me?*

The fact that nature ensures relatively equal exchanges of benefit is why attractive people are seldom in relationships with unattractive people and when they are we naturally wonder what hidden quality the other person has that is equally desirable. We instinctively recognize that for relationships to form, though they don't have to be of like kind, nature ensures that the benefits being exchanged be of equal value.

The divorce rate in this country is about fifty percent, which we consciously perceive as being poor. And there is no end to the debate over whom and what is to blame. But from nature's perspective, this number is of no consequence because it isn't marriage that benefits our species; it's healthy relationships. This is why, though many religious organizations think that making divorce difficult improves society, it actually has quite the opposite effect. Only healthy relationships benefit the group, and people don't need to be coerced to stay in healthy relationships; nature impels it. Leveraging a person's acceptance to artificially sustain an unhealthy relationship only adds to the dysfunction. The reason it's so much easier to get married than to stay married is that marriage is a conscious construct that, even though it facilitates many of society's needs, it seldom, if ever, fully satisfies nature's needs. To get married, we have but to satisfy a rather simplistic set of superficial criteria that we have consciously created. But to remain married, we must meet the very real and complex needs of nature. This is why, regardless of any vows at the altar, divorces, separations, and desertions still happen. It is not such conscious commitments, but rather nature and the relationship's ability to provide mutual benefits, which determines when it will begin and end.

WHEN THE BENEFITS GO NOT TO OURSELVES, BUT TO OUR SPECIES

Intricate as they may be, the relationships that benefit us personally are not our most perplexing. That title goes to the relationships that serve to benefit our species. To understand most of our relationships we have but to recognize what we as individuals get out of them. But to understand our relationships with infants or the unborn, we must understand how our behaviors benefit the species, which is not something we're used to doing. Because these relationships are not prompted by self-benefit, but rather by the instinctual need to ensure the survival of the next generation, the feelings they evoke are different than those of other relationships. This is why it's so difficult to remain objective when considering such issues as abortion, embryo screening, stem cell research, and sometimes even contraception. From our conscious perspective, we're not just trying to rationally weigh how such things might affect us and our acceptance, we're doing so amidst a profusion of irrational promptings intended to further our species, impulses that are foreign to the conscious mind.

Think about what it is that makes us care about another person. It isn't the tangible existence of their body; it's their personality and character. So when we find ourselves caring even more about our young before they develop such qualities, to make sense of it, again, we fill in the blanks with our own consciously imagined explanations. This is the essence of why abortion is such a contentious issue. Instead of objectively seeing the fetus as it is, an early form of life with virtually no conscious capabilities, we project our own such capabilities onto them and envision a personality that would warrant such feelings. This is why we so often become emphatic and unyielding in our position on such issues. Because we lack the ability to objectively unpack all those feelings, we find it comforting to adopt a delusion of certainty regarding why we experience them, a delusion that often becomes manifest in the practice of religion.

10

Belief vs. Self-delusion, Our Most Harmful Confusion

Another of our top ten most misused words is belief. Because we have yet to grasp how beliefs are formed, and we seldom recognize when we are deceiving ourselves, we often misuse the word to describe things we merely wish we believed. A lot of the things we think we believe are not beliefs at all, but rather desirable self-delusions, which makes this chapter of particular importance when trying to understand the practice of religion.

THE CATEGORICAL DIFFERENCE BETWEEN A BELIEF AND A SELF-DELUSION

To understand the often imperceptible distinction between a belief and a self-delusion, we have but to understand how each comes to exist. A belief is merely our conscious recognition of something we have instinctually determined to be true or real. A self-delusion is the self-induced distortion of such a determination. The noteworthy difference is that, because our instinctual processes take place upstream of the conscious mind, we have no control over the things we believe. We only have control over how we subsequently distort our instinctual determinations (i.e., our self-delusions).

A belief is, by definition, confidence that something is true or real, a feeling that only materializes when we instinctually determine that such is the case. It comprises a chemical change that is genetically triggered when our instinctive processes perceive that something actually exists or has occurred. Consequently, no matter how much we might want to, we cannot willfully choose, alter, or manipulate the things we believe. Because we only become aware of our feelings after they have been produced, like those of trust and respect, we have no conscious say in them. This is why the term *make-believe* means pretend or imaginary. It is quite literally impossible to *make* ourselves *believe* anything. If our unconscious instinctive processes do not determine that something is true or real, they will not trigger the chemical changes that constitute a belief, in which case all we can do is delude ourselves with the pretense of a belief. Hence the definition of self-delusion being a self-induced false belief held in the face of strong evidence to the contrary, a self-created distortion of what we have instinctually determined to be true and real.

The sole reason we distort our instinctual perceptions is to feel better. Our self-delusions serve as a kind of psychological workaround that enables us to improve how we feel without having to improve our circumstance, a very attractive, but often harmful, shortcut to feeling better immediately. When reality is discomforting, we have two choices. We can embrace it and be uncomfortable in the here and now, or we can reject it, delude ourselves with an altered, more comforting version of reality, and deal with the ongoing conflicts that result from a distorted perspective. It's essentially nature's version of pay me now or pay me later, for when it comes to uncomfortable realities there is no free lunch. The all too common result is that, because our instinctual focus is dominated by how we feel in the present and we don't always recognize the longer-term consequences of succumbing to it, we often choose the latter at the expense of our future.

The distinction between belief and self-delusion often goes unrealized because not only do we not yet recognize that beliefs are entirely involuntary, but our self-delusions are basically a shortcut to many similar emotional effects. A belief causes us to feel better because it reflects instinctive certainty, while self-delusion does so through a pretense of certainty. The more uncomfortable our circumstance, the more disposed we become to distorting reality and embracing it as real. Thus the old saying "there are no atheists in a foxhole." We use self-delusion as a kind of coping mechanism to escape life's harsher realities, such as the imminent threat to life that soldiers often face in the midst of battle. This is why in severe accidents or crimes, eyewitness testimony is consistently revealed to be less reliable than objective forms of evidence such as video. We instinctively employ our imaginations to create a more psychologically palatable version of events.

Because we instinctually fear the unknown, that natural discomfort plays a significant role in prompting our self-delusions. This is why words such as *know* and *knowledge* also rank among our most misused. The discomfort of not knowing makes it emotionally attractive to go beyond what we know, imagine an explanation, and embrace it as knowledge. This is the basic process by which virtually all our misconceptions come to exist. We create our own kind of faux knowledge to receive the comfort it can provide.

The fact that our beliefs are but a conscious manifestation of our instinctual perceptions is what makes self-delusion intrinsic to the term faith. The definition of faith is belief not based on proof, something that cannot and does not occur. Because our beliefs are merely a different form of our instinctual determinations, they cannot and do not materialize absent the proof of the physical things that triggered them. Faith is a kind of single-word oxymoron we have created to embody our unrealistic desire to consciously choose the things we believe. When someone says you must have faith, what they are actually saying is that because there is no proof that can or will result in a belief, if you want to feel better you must pretend that you believe. As Samuel Langhorne Clemens, better known as Mark Twain, wrote, "Faith is believing what you know ain't so."[17] This is the ever so dangerous purpose of faith: to convince ourselves of notions for which there is no proof. Faith represents not belief, but rather a pretense of belief, for the purpose of improving how we feel.

WHY ABSOLUTELY NO ONE BELIEVES IN GOD

Because we determine truth and reality instinctively from our experiences, our beliefs are by nature limited to the physical things that comprise those experiences. Our genetic instructions do not trigger any such feeling of confidence about the nonphysical or supernatural because we do not detect such things with our senses. Any notion we may have of something nonphysical or supernatural must be created with imagination, a seemingly subtle distinction from our conscious perspective, but one of paramount importance to the instinctual processes that determine our behaviors to ensure our survival.

The basic reality that we do not form beliefs regarding anything nonphysical can be seen in the fact that no one, not even the devoutly religious, is anxious to die. Though we consciously envision such things as God and heaven, we subconsciously know that there is nothing among our physical experiences that demonstrates they exist. If our instinctual processes determined that some ultimate paradise awaited us after death, they would produce the feeling of being eager to experience it. But of course we experience no such feeling when it comes to dying. That's not to say that people don't embrace the false notion of a belief to rationalize taking life. But it is to say that one must significantly distort their instinctual determinations, to achieve such a mindset.

The feeling we commonly misinterpret as a religious belief is actually that of self-delusion, the comforting effects produced by deceiving ourselves into thinking that we believe. Because actual beliefs are by nature not possible regarding the supernatural, the term *religious belief* is but another yet to be recognized oxymoron. Incredible as it may seem, and in spite of all claims to the contrary, no one past the age of about six or seven actually believes in any kind of God or heaven, not even the devoutly religious. Yes, let me type that again. No matter how inconceivable it may be from a religious perspective, the categorical reality is that no adolescent or adult actually believes in God. Once we've developed the mental wherewithal to determine truth and reality ourselves, we are genetically compelled to do so, a biological reality that necessarily limits our beliefs to the physical things and events that make up our experiences. This is why, even if we are raised from birth to be very religious, at the age of about six or seven we invariably begin to question, at least to ourselves, what we've been told about God and heaven. That's when we begin relying on our own instinctual perceptions. And no matter how uncomfortable it may make us to realize that we lack any religious beliefs, there is nothing we can do to change that reality. Our only alternative is to delude ourselves with the false notion of such a belief, which is precisely what a great many of us do to receive the comfort it provides. In the words of the 18th-century Scottish philosopher and historian David Hume, "Men dare not avow, even to their own hearts, the doubts which they entertain on such subjects."[18]

The fact that no one possesses a religious belief is why people feel the need to attend church. Any pretense of knowledge or belief regarding the supernatural is continually conflicting with our instinctual determinations, which prompts the constant need for affirmation. Think about it; even though we can't see it or touch it, we don't feel any need to hold a school on gravity every Sunday. Because gravity is a physical phenomenon with consistent repeatable effects, we have instinctually determined that it is real. This is why, even though the consequences of ignoring gravity may pale in comparison to those of ignoring an omniscient, omnipotent Supreme Being, everyone considers gravity in everything they do. Unlike the supernatural, we possess a belief in gravity's omnipresent existence. As much as we might enjoy the notion of a religious text causing us to believe, nature ensures that it plays no such role. Because putting our imaginings on paper doesn't make them any more real, such texts are of no consequence to the unconscious processes that discern truth and reality.

HOW SELF-DELUSION CAN BE SO HARMFUL

We use truth in three principal ways. We determine it about our environment, which makes our reactions more efficient and effective. We employ it selectively as a tool, which affords us maximum benefit from our relationships. And we effectively ration it to ourselves to regulate our level of comfort. But because that last use adversely affects the first two, it is by far the most important (i.e., it matters little how well we discern reality or interact with others if we end up distorting it to ourselves).

Because we naturally shape our self-delusions to satisfy our emotional needs, they are always necessarily unique to ourselves. Consequently, to the degree we create such shortcuts to comfort, our picture of reality becomes not just distorted and invalid, but assured of conflicting with truth, reality, and everyone else's unique such creations. This is how our self-deceptions spawn our most horrific conflicts. When we use them to ease our greatest discomforts, our self-delusions quickly become emotionally indispensable.

Because we are always at least subconsciously aware that our self-deceptions are not supported by reality, and therefore cannot be rationally explained or defended, we are never entirely at ease with them. This is why emotion and conflicts are somewhat intrinsic to politics and religion. Both of these subjects occasion considerable self-delusions. And because it enhances our comfort to feel certain, those delusions are not just rationally untenable, they become largely inflexible. Because politics and religion are all about our hopes and fears, we invariably view them not as they are but rather as we wish them to be, and then become intransigent in our position. This is why when people discuss these subjects they often don't so much listen, as just wait to talk. They have long since formed an image that provides them comfort and are no longer interested in or receptive to further information that might jeopardize it. Hence the old saying, "If you want to keep your friends your friends, never discuss politics or religion." When it comes to these subjects, self-delusion often dominates our perspective.

A rather significant though seldom noticed harm of self-delusion is that it diminishes our ability to interact with others. Though we each possess an enormous capacity to be kind, helpful, and generous, we only exhibit such qualities on occasion. The primary reason is that, by nature, we only consider helping others to the extent we feel at ease with ourselves; a state of being that becomes compromised by the tenuous nature of self-delusion. The more we distort our instinctual perceptions, the more self-absorbed we become with reconciling the internal conflicts it creates. This is why genuinely nice people so often possess both the desire and the ability to help others. The same unvarnished perspective that enables them to recognize and deal with reality in an unaltered state also affords them the equipoise and emotional capacity to reach out to those in need. The significance being, there is virtually no limit to how much better we can live and feel by abandoning our self-delusions and embracing reality.

The most elemental harm of achieving our comfort through self-deception is that it undermines the very function of our feelings. Because the purpose of our feelings is to prompt and guide our behaviors, when we take such psychological shortcuts to feeling better, we effectively circumvent the genetic mechanism that is meant to ensure our survival, a practice that occasions considerable harmful consequences. Because self-delusion provides a psychological cause to do nothing or, worse yet, to do the wrong thing in place of taking beneficial action, not only does it allow our circumstances to grow worse, our comfort then becomes dependent on ever more self-deceptions. It's a lot like taking a painkiller. Though it improves how we feel, it doesn't address the problem. And because it makes it so easy to feel better, it often leads to an addiction.

Though self-delusion is not commonly recognized for or classified in terms of its addictive properties, it is arguably our most powerful, harmful, and pervasive habit. Not only is it always readily available, but unlike drugs or alcohol, we don't realize when we're using it. Since we don't have to buy or ingest anything, self-delusion enables us to instantly improve how we feel without ever becoming aware of what we are doing. Such is the essence of self-delusion: it enables us to feel better by keeping the deception from the conscious mind. And since we don't correlate the behavior with its consequences, unlike other addictions, self-delusion never produces any kind of rock-bottom event that would make us want to quit.

When we act on a false belief as if it were a legitimate belief, because we're treating something we've imagined as if it were real, there are always consequences. And when we do this to ease a substantial discomfort, those consequences can be lethal. It all comes down to how much we need comfort and how we have been conditioned to obtain it. This is why some religious people refuse medical treatment. It's not that they don't know what science can do; it's that they feel such a desperate need to sustain their pretense of religious belief that they are willing to risk their own life or that of a loved one, to do so.

Perhaps the most harmful aspect of self-delusion, however, is its inherent compounding nature. When we choose the immediate comfort of a false belief, we distort our picture of reality, which in turn necessitates that we distort subsequent experiences, to sustain that comfort, a burden that grows ever larger with time. This is why when we hear someone described as eccentric we naturally envision someone older. We intuitively recognize that our distortions compound, and therefore become more pronounced over time. It's another reason why being truthful with our children is so fundamentally important. Though our own immediate comfort is always vying to be served, the harm of denying children reality early in life continues to compound for as long as they live. It's a large part of why young people are more receptive to new ways of thinking. They don't yet have a lot of emotional equity tied up in falsehoods, which leaves them better able to recognize and accept things as they actually are.

RECOGNIZING OUR SELF-DELUSIONS

Our natural propensity is to deny the existence of our self-delusions, even when others point them out. As the 16th-century playwright John Heywood put it, "There are none so blind as those who will not see. The most deluded people are those who choose to ignore what they already know."[19] This is why we sometimes, without explanation, simply refuse to further discuss something. It's not that we've been caught in a lie. If we get trapped in a lie, it's rather easy to mount a defense with further lies. But when reality corners one of our self-deceptions, it often obliterates our entire perspective, leaving us completely defenseless. So we choose to withdraw rather than advance a conversation that can only hasten the discomfort we were trying to avoid.

What makes it difficult to discern when we are deceiving ourselves is the fact that, though self-delusions are always false beliefs, false beliefs are not always self-delusions. False beliefs can occur accidentally, from invalid information or flawed reasoning. There is, however, a discernible difference between purposeful and accidental false beliefs. False beliefs that result from a mistaken understanding often appear to concur with surrounding realities, hence the mistake. While false beliefs that are self-induced, because their sole function is to depart from the real, generally contrast with surrounding realities. We can often tell when we are deluding ourselves by simply recognizing when we are rejecting realities. It's more easily said than done, but possible nonetheless. This is how and why when a politician is caught lying or an athlete caught cheating, those who have no particular interest in them can easily recognize the offence, while those who support that politician or athlete find it somewhat impossible. Again, we tend to reject realities that diminish our delusions, even when they are obvious to everyone else.

Another way to discern when we are deceiving ourselves is to impose consequences for being wrong. Because we are always subconsciously aware of our self-deceptions, and our sole instinctual objective is to acquire benefit, we can expose our self-delusions to the conscious mind by attaching risk to our position. For instance, we can delude ourselves into thinking we believe that heaven exists and offers a much better experience than life on Earth. But when we ask ourselves if we are eager to die to experience it, it quickly becomes apparent that we don't actually believe in heaven: we just wish it to be true.

Because our beliefs are merely a conscious manifestation of a subconscious event, unlike our self-delusions, they naturally get reflected in our behaviors. This is why when we do something that we know is wrong, our natural immediate concern is not how God views it, but rather whether anyone saw us do it. We have instinctually determined that the consequences, if any, will come not from the supernatural but from fellow human beings. If we actually believed that an all-knowing, all-powerful being was using the things we do, to determine our fate for the rest of eternity, it would instinctually dominate our concerns and be overwhelmingly evident in all of our behaviors. But of course that is not the case, not even for the most devout practitioners. If someone's immediate response to any behavior is concern over how God perceives it, objectively speaking, it indicates a very strong and broad distortion of reality. Fortunately, when most of us ponder the potential religious ramifications of our actions, it generally takes place well after the fact and at our own emotional convenience.

11

Our Exclusively Human Thirst for Religion

Because we can only become aware of physical phenomena, any guess we might make regarding the supernatural must be completely blind. We must rely entirely on our imagination to create the things it comprises. The inescapable effect being, to embrace religion, we find ourselves having to ignore, distort, or reject all the instinctual determinations that conflict with those imaginings. This chapter explains our most widespread misperceptions and debunks the most common self-deceptions generated by our desire for religion.

If a behavior's significance is measured by its effects, then few things approach our human practice of religion. Throughout time religion has played a prominent role in humanity's most destructive conflicts. Accordingly, if every person was somehow granted the answer to a single question, for a great many that question would be "Does God exist?" But since we are precluded by nature from knowing such things, the real question is why do we want so strongly for the answer to be yes? Why do we go beyond the bounds of truth and knowledge to answer that question in the affirmative? Only by answering this question can we understand our most enigmatic and misconstrued human behavior: religion.

WHAT RELIGION DOES FOR US

Whenever a behavior can be found around the world and throughout history, it's a safe bet that it satisfies some kind of instinctual need, and the human practice of religion is a great example. Because our feelings are the means by which our genetic instructions effect our survival, we experience none stronger than those surrounding our apprehension of death, which are precisely the feelings that religion addresses. We are unique in that we are the first species to experience these powerful genetic compulsions to survive while at the same time knowing we are going to die, creating an innate conflict the magnitude of which is unparalleled throughout nature. Religion is not any kind of neurological disorder as some have half-jokingly suggested, it is a kind of self-induced psychosis we have developed to deal with this greatest of all instinctual discomforts.

When it comes to death, our easiest and sometimes only way of easing the psychological discomfort it evokes is to adopt a perspective that escapes its harsh reality. Again, this is the predominant function of our imagination: to envision things that make us feel better. This is why people embrace religion more as they get older. Though not always perceptible at the conscious level, we become more discomforted as our eventual demise commands a larger presence on the horizon.

Religion serves as a considerable conditional source of comfort. It can improve how we feel, but only to the extent we suspend truth and reality. This is why it isn't our intelligence, but rather how we were conditioned to obtain comfort as a child, that determines whether or not we practice religion as an adult. Because our most elemental priority is comfort, if we have been conditioned to obtain it through a pretense of supernatural knowledge, we will use our intelligence not to better discern truth and reality in the face of discomfort, but to better rationalize the self-delusions that help us escape discomfort. This is why even geniuses not just practice religion, but develop bad habits and addictions. It's not that they lack the intelligence to understand what they're doing. It's that their intelligence becomes utilized to rationalize the behaviors that provide them comfort. Because the way we are habituated to deal with discomfort early in life determines how we use our intelligence, it is a crucial fork in the road that determines who we become and how much we accomplish throughout life.

THE GENESIS OF RELIGION

Religion exists in many different forms because the need it satisfies emerged with our conscious capabilities, back when our ancestors were still living in isolated groups. As they became increasingly aware of their own mortality, each tribe had to come up with its own way of coping with that greatest of all discomforts. The inevitable result being, each group imagined a scenario in which life somehow continued. This is why there are roughly as many religions as there are languages. Our species acquired the need for both relatively early in its conscious development, necessitating that each isolated community create its own solutions. The notable difference, of course, is that language satisfies a practical need, while religion satisfies an emotional need.

It's also not just a coincidence that each isolated community arrived at some type of God as the answer to their unknowns. Only recently have we begun to understand the chemistry and physics behind how things come to exist and occur naturally. Thousands of years ago, the only conceivable method was through a purposeful act, making it not just natural but inevitable that each group would imagine some type of much wiser mythical being as having created the things they didn't understand.

WHY RELIGIOUS VIEWS CHANGE OVER TIME

Whether or not we can see it from our individual perspectives, mankind is well down the path of becoming one large group. All those once small isolated groups have grown, producing a collision of cultures that is forcing us to reconcile our various indigenous differences. The difficulty being, each group brings with it not just its rational knowledge, but its irrational ways of dealing with life's unknowns. Our success in coming together on a global scale is fundamentally dependent on our ability to address these differences, both rational and irrational. To the extent our differences are of a rational nature, we merely have to recognize their mutual truths and realities. This is why we have little trouble translating languages; they are but different terms for the same real things. But to the degree our differences are of an irrational nature, because they are each unique, they cannot be reconciled. All we can do is hope for somewhat similar imaginings, a seemingly subtle distinction of enormous consequence.

Our religious perspectives do not differ and conflict because some people know more about the supernatural than others, for no one possesses any such knowledge. Religious perspectives differ and conflict because we each imagine them to satisfy our own personal needs. This is why, though countless millions can read the same religious text, no two people ever come away with the same understanding. We each have different emotional needs. This is how religion fundamentally stymies the process of coming together and living in peace. There is no reconciling behaviors the rationale for which is a unique emotionally shaped creation of each person's mind. And because our religious imaginings serve to ease our strongest instinctual discomforts, not only are they the ultimate tool for manipulation, but the conflicts they generate are among the most violent in nature.

Religion is ever so gradually waning because our instinctual desire to coexist is constantly pressuring us to purge our most irrational and conflict-ridden behaviors. The fact that religion isn't declining any faster than it is speaks to the vital role that comfort plays in effecting our survival. Because comfort is our most elemental priority, we will not give up our most expedient means of achieving it until we begin to recognize the harm that comes from taking such shortcuts. We will not relinquish our delusions of supernatural knowledge, dismiss our myths, legends, fables, and folklore, or cease practicing such pseudosciences as voodoo, witchcraft, and prayer, until we comprehend how such things actually preclude a peaceful coexistence. When it comes to prayer, we know that it doesn't increase the likelihood of a favorable outcome. But it's part of the delusion we impose on ourselves, to receive the comfort that religion can provide. Perhaps 19th-century American writer Ambrose Bierce said it best in his *Devil's Dictionary*, where under the word "Pray" he wrote: "To ask that the laws of the universe be annulled in behalf of a single petitioner confessedly unworthy."[20]

HOW AND WHY RELIGION AND REASON ARE MUTUALLY EXCLUSIVE

Religion is by its very nature the only commonly embraced human behavior that is both inherently averse to and necessarily devoid of reason. At the heart of this incontrovertible reality is the fact that we cannot apply the processes of logic or reason to things of which we have no knowledge, a category that encompasses everything nonphysical or supernatural. Though it might seem as though we are employing logic and reason, any conclusions drawn from imagined constituents also necessitate the process of imagining. This is the essence of self-delusion: we convince ourselves that our imagined explanations are a product of logic and reason.

To recognize religion's irrational nature, we have but to juxtapose it with rational human behavior. For instance, when a number of people become sick with the same symptoms, from say food poisoning or disease, without question or hesitation we seek out the precise nature and source of the cause, to preclude further harm. For the same reason, we keep exhaustive data on the safety of products and services. Whenever human life is at risk in any way, we do everything we can to set aside our emotions and deal with it in an objective rational manner. We do this across-the-board in every situation and circumstance save one: our practice of religion. When it comes to our most prolific agent of death, destruction, and terrorism, not only do we make no effort to study and understand its causal relationships, we have enacted and actually hold dear laws that ensure we are able to continue the practice, demonstrating perhaps the ultimate in irrational behaviors.

In spite of being our most harmful behavior, religion is the only behavior we have made expressly exempt from the edifying scrutiny of truth and reality. As a species, we have made the incredible leap to possess a conscious awareness, far and away the single most significant development in life on Earth. Yet when we practice religion, we effectively discard its immeasurable benefits. Because the actual function of religion is to improve how we feel, people the world over are quite happy to adamantly insist on practicing their own brand without the slightest understanding of how it affects their behavior. The underlying reason is that we know, at least subconsciously, that if we conducted any type of objective investigation into how and why religion is linked to so much harm it would become evident that it is entirely irrational, a realization that would make religion considerably more difficult to embrace as a source of comfort. In the words of Thomas Paine, "It is error only, and not truth, that shrinks from inquiry."[21]

One rather ubiquitous sign that religion is an irrational source of comfort is that we only credit our positive experiences to it. Athletes only point to the sky when they catch the ball, not when they drop it. It doesn't behoove us to diminish our illusionary source of comfort. This is why miracles are always of a positive nature. Though we no doubt experience just as many rare bad events as good ones, we never describe the bad ones as miraculous. We selectively ascribe only positive experiences to divine intervention. In the words of the 18th-century philosopher, writer, and American Revolutionary War hero Ethan Allen, "In those parts of the world where learning and science has prevailed, miracles have ceased; but in such parts of it as are barbarous and ignorant, miracles are still in vogue."[22] Or as Mark Twain once quipped, "There is nothing more awe-inspiring than a miracle except the credulity that can take it at par."[23]

Religion exists as our most enigmatic behavior because we must necessarily abandon logic and reason to engage in it. Unlike the process of understanding, which is fundamentally dependent on truth and reality, religion is dependent on our imagination creating a complete departure from truth and reality. In a study conducted on religion at the University of British Columbia in Vancouver[24], psychologists William Gervais and Ara Norenzayan found that people who think more analytically were less likely to be religious, while people who approach problems more intuitively were more likely to be religious. The correlation being, analytical thinking involves the conscious processes of logic and reason, while intuitive solutions are derived from what we feel, absent logic and reason. It's why a meta-analysis of 63 studies published in *Personality and Social Psychology Review*[25] showed a markedly negative association between intelligence and religiosity (i.e., there is a worldwide inverse correlation between such rational attributes as education and intelligence, and the irrational practice of religion). This reality is even further evidenced by a WIN/Gallup International poll[26] that showed a global inverse correlation between religiosity and income. The more cognizant we are of factual reality, the less plausible such imaginings appear, the less need we feel to embrace them as knowledge, the more rational we behave, and the more successful we become in most anything we do.

Many theologians and philosophers throughout the ages have recognized and captured this intrinsic antithetical relationship between religion and reason. The 16th-century German theologian and Augustinian monk Martin Luther wrote, "Reason is the greatest enemy that faith has; it never comes to the aid of spiritual things, but — more frequently than not — struggles against the divine Word, treating with contempt all that emanates from God."[27] For religion to enhance our comfort we must function in the realm of the imagined and pretend to know that which we cannot. The 18th-century French philosopher, Denis Diderot, addressed this when he wrote, "The philosopher has never killed any priests, whereas the priest has killed a great many philosophers."[28] As quoted in the book *Breaking The Spell*[29], "Philosophy is questions that may never be answered. Religion is answers that may never be questioned."

WHEN WE INFER KNOWLEDGE FROM WHAT WE DO NOT KNOW

In the words of Isaac Newton, "What we know is a drop, what we don't know is an ocean."[30] The problem is that when the complexity of something exceeds our ability to understand, because we are instinctually discomforted by the unknown, we often create our own explanation and embrace it as knowledge. And for those who have been habituated to the practice of religion, those explanations often take the same all-inclusive form: that it's the work of God, hence the need for such incontestable catchall rationalizations as "God works in mysterious ways." In reality, because our inability to understand something in no way indicates how it came to exist or occur, such reasoning is unequivocally invalid. It merely transforms our uncomfortable ignorance about the physical into a more comfortable faux knowledge about the nonphysical, paving a direct path to conflict.

When we create and embrace supernatural explanations, we do so without any kind of rational logic or reason and in spite of all knowledge to the contrary. We must completely discount the gargantuan fact that, without exception, every single thing and event that mankind has ever come to understand has proven to be not just of a physical nature, but the natural and necessary result of the physical things and events that preceded it. We must ignore the ubiquitous reality that, if our extensive past is any indication, everything we currently attribute to the nonphysical or supernatural will in time be shown to be an entirely physical effect of an entirely physical cause. To quote Albert Einstein, "All our science, measured against reality, is primitive and childlike — and yet it is the most precious thing we have."[31]

One of the most common justifications given for subscribing to religion is the inability to fathom how life and our universe could come to exist if there was no God. But the reality of how such things came to exist is entirely unrelated to our awareness. No matter how aware we are or become, our ability to comprehend represents nothing more than the awareness of a single species of life, on a single planet, in a single solar system, in a single galaxy, in an immensely vast universe, at a particular point in time. As psychologically comforting and convenient as it may be, the notion that we can use our limited and constantly changing human awareness as some kind of benchmark from which to conclude that there must be a God is not only illogical and invalid, it is naively arrogant. Though we may be the most aware species on planet Earth, when it comes to our universe, astronomers have already found that there are likely more than 40 billion Earth-size planets in our galaxy alone that orbit a star and are in what scientists refer to as the not-too-hot and not-too-cold "Goldilocks Zone" for supporting life[32]. Assuming our galaxy to be of average size, when you multiply that by the estimated 100 billion galaxies in the *observable* universe, you get a staggering number of potentially habitable planets: four sextillion. That means it is possible that 4,000,000,000,000,000,000,000 planets could sustain life. And that doesn't include the possibility of untold other universes, a possibility that many physicists are now seriously considering, and one that could add a great many zeroes to the end of that number.

Though we tend to perceive ourselves as the be-all and end-all of conscious knowledge, we are but an infinitesimally small element of an incomprehensibly vast universe. That which seems inexplicable to our species at this particular point in time may well be blatantly obvious to innumerable other forms of life, a reality that makes our lack of knowledge completely valueless in determining the existence of a God. Yet, for the sake of our comfort, we often use what we don't know, to affirm God's existence. In the words of the 16th-century French writer Michel de Montaigne: "[Man] cannot make a worm, yet he will make gods by the dozen."[33] Every piece of factual data ever collected indicates that the only correlation between complexity and its intentional creation is one of inverse proportion. But because our limited awareness precludes us from grasping how something as complex as life or as vast as the universe could come to exist naturally, we commonly ignore this considerable reality and ascribe such things to the work of a Supreme Being.

THE ORIGINAL INTENT OF A CHRISTIAN NATION

Perhaps the most common misperception regarding the creation of this country is that it was intended to be a Christian nation. That was not what the founding fathers wanted or intended, which becomes abundantly clear when we look at our nation's two most notable documents, the Declaration of Independence and the Constitution, in the context of their very different purposes.

What many people don't realize about the Declaration of Independence is that it is not any kind of binding or governing document. It was created to outline a moral case that would enlist support for breaking away from Great Britain; that's all. Its purpose was to rally both secular and religious rationales during a time when kings claimed to rule nations by the authority of God. As The Declaration of Independence expressly states, it was based on the idea that "Governments are instituted among Men, deriving their just powers from the consent of the governed," which was a radical departure from governments of that time. The use of such artful terms as creator, nature's God, or divine providence in the Declaration of Independence is to be expected, as the intent of this nonbinding document was to enlist the support of a mostly religious audience.

In sharp contrast to the Declaration of Independence, the Constitution is a document that was created for the express purpose of defining the lawful rules by which our nation would be governed. Had the founding fathers in any way wanted or intended this country to be a Christian or otherwise religious nation, they would have manifested that intention in this purposefully binding document. But our Constitution contains absolutely no mention of any terms even remotely resembling creator, God, or divine. Quite to the contrary, the only two mentions of religion are averse to it, specifically mandating that government take no role in it and that it never be a requirement for holding public office.

For anyone who might still have doubts regarding the intended role of Christianity or religion in this country's affairs, perhaps nowhere is it made any clearer than in the treaty with Tripoli of Barbary. The terms and conditions of that agreement, which was drafted in 1796 under the Presidency of George Washington and signed in 1797 by succeeding President John Adams, unequivocally state that "no pretext arising from religious opinions shall ever produce an interruption of the harmony existing between the two countries" and that "the Government of the United States of America is not, in any sense, founded on the Christian religion." Perhaps even more telling is the fact that this wording caused no discord with politicians or the public. The undeniable reality being, no matter how anyone tries to spin it today, this country was not founded as or ever intended to be a Christian nation.

OUR GOVERNMENT'S IMPLICIT ENDORSEMENT OF RELIGION

A somewhat natural effect of religion being popular amongst the citizens is that, in spite of it violating the Constitution, our government encourages it. By making religious groups exempt from taxes, our government doesn't just give them a financial preference over nonreligious organizations and thereby encourage irrational behaviors, those who behave rationally must pay higher taxes to make up for it. In the words of the 19th-century author, poet, and philosopher Henry David Thoreau, "I did not see why the schoolmaster should be taxed to support the priest, and not the priest the schoolmaster."[34] Perhaps even more poignant were the words of our third president, Thomas Jefferson, who in 1786 wrote regarding religious freedom, "To compel a man to furnish contributions of money for the propagation of opinions which he disbelieves and abhors is sinful and tyrannical."[35] But that's exactly what our government is doing.

Most people think that religious groups are given tax-exempt status because they are charities. But in fact, our government doesn't treat them like charities; it treats them much better. In what can only be interpreted as an effort to encourage religion, our government specifically singles out religious organizations and expressly exempts them from the stringent financial transparency rules that all other nonprofits must follow. The net effect is that, because they don't have to account for the monies they take in, churches don't have to act charitable. They're able to simply amass wealth without paying any taxes, which makes them a magnet for abuse and exploitation. But because religion is popular, people readily ignore this overt violation of our Constitution and cheerfully continue giving them money.

To give some measure to just how blatantly we disregard the Constitution when it comes to religion, at the time of this writing, seven of our 50 states (Arkansas, Maryland, Mississippi, North Carolina, South Carolina, Tennessee, and Texas) still had laws that make it illegal to run for public office if one does not believe in some kind of God. Even though these state laws exist in direct conflict with Article VI, paragraph 3 of the U.S. Constitution, which states "No religious test shall ever be required as a qualification to any office or public trust under the United States," they remain on the books. It's a stark reminder of how, when it comes to the separation of Church and State, our judicial system often looks the other way.

A somewhat natural effect of thinking that religion improves behavior is the mistaken notion that people in predominantly non-religious countries are less moral. This was perhaps the greatest falsehood our government repeatedly professed in large-scale propaganda campaigns aimed at enlisting support against "those godless communists" during the Cold War. But because religion does not improve behavior, it merely served as a means of manipulating the masses, just as it has in countless other countries throughout the ages. It's the same type of irrational premise that governments used to enlist support for the Crusades, the Medieval Inquisitions, the Spanish Inquisitions, the Portuguese Inquisitions, the Roman Inquisitions, the witch trials, and the severe oppression of such leading thinkers as da Vinci, Copernicus, and Galileo. As 18th-century French historian and philosopher Francois-Marie Arouet, better known by his pen name of Voltaire, once said, "Those who can make you believe absurdities can make you commit atrocities."[36]

Though we like to think of religious atrocities as a thing of the past, the reality is they still occur globally on a daily basis. The dismissal of reason that paves a shortcut to comfort still marshals rationalizations for hatred, discrimination, persecution, starvation, torture, and murder around the world. There isn't a single life on Earth that hasn't been shortened and made more difficult by irrational behavior, behavior that religion produces on the largest of scales. This is how and why many of the most religious countries are home to the most deplorable human rights records and are involved in the most horrific conflicts; irrational thinking is strongly embraced by the populace. Until we recognize that the fundamental problem is our willingness to embrace imagined pretenses as an acceptable rationale for human behavior, religion will continue to reign supreme as the ultimate generator of death, destruction, and terrorism, our government will continue to endorse it, and we will fail miserably in our attempts to rein in its incessant conflicts.

RELIGION AMONGST THE FOIBLES OF OUR SUPREME COURT

The method by which we select our Supreme Court justices effectively ensures they possess a religious bias. Because they have to be confirmed by representatives of the people, who have been and continue to be predominantly religious, if a nominee is not religious, it is somewhat of a political certainty that they will not be selected. This is why, even though it violates the Constitution, the motto In God We Trust hangs on the wall of the Supreme Court. The Court's affinity for religion is but an outgrowth of how a majority of citizens feel about it.

Whether one is encouraged or depressed by the thought of it, our Supreme Court represents the leading edge of mankind's effort to become ever more rational and objective in dealing with societal matters. But even Supreme Court justices have human fallibilities and deny themselves reality when they experience enough need, something that is perhaps most easily seen in their rulings regarding the phrase In God We Trust. By allowing this phrase to become our national motto and be printed on our currency, our courts have, to put it respectfully, perpetrated one of greatest legal stretches in our country's history.

When it comes to our government's involvement in religion, the Constitution is concise and absolute. The Establishment Clause of the First Amendment states "Congress shall make no law respecting an establishment of religion, or prohibiting the free exercise thereof." The word "respecting" meant the same thing then as it does today: regarding, concerning, touching upon, or relating to. The First Amendment prohibits government from exerting any influence for or against religion, which the Supreme Court unequivocally confirmed in the 1962 landmark case *Engel v. Vitale* with the declaration that even nondenominational school prayer was unconstitutional because a prayer by any definition constitutes a religious activity. The significance being, to rule on whether or not our government's use of the phrase In God We Trust was constitutional, the Court merely had to determine whether or not it was in any way religious.

On three separate occasions, in 1970 ("*Aronow v. United States*," 432 F.2d 242), 1979 ("*Madalyn Murray O'Hair, et al. v. W. Michael Blumenthal, Secretary of Treasury, et al.*" 588 F.2d 1144), and 1994 ("*Freedom From Religion Foundation v. United States*," 74 F.3d 214), federal courts found our government's use of the phrase In God We Trust to be constitutional. And each time, the Supreme Court did what it so often does when it wants to avoid a problematic issue: it refused to hear the appeal. It characterized its opinion as "consistent with the proposition that government may not communicate an endorsement of religious belief." In each of these cases the court's position was that the motto is an example of *ceremonial deism*, a legal term for religious statements that are deemed to have lost their religious content due to longtime customary use. And on the surface that might sound reasonable, for one would like to think that our Supreme Court justices had a sound legal basis on which to make such a ruling. But there are two glaring problems with the ceremonial deism rationale. One, it's an admission that prior to the phrase losing its religious content it was in fact unconstitutional. And two, the phrase has not lost its religious content, which poses increasing legal, ethical, political, and popularity problems for these judges.

The fact that religious meaning is the very essence of In God We Trust is why those who support its use and those who oppose it are so markedly divided along religious lines. No matter how or how long one uses the term God, it still only has one meaning: a religious deity. If prayer is, as the Supreme Court has ruled, religious by its very nature, then by Justice Scalia's reduction to the absurd form of argument, the term God must certainly be religious. In other words, it would be absurd for people to pray to God if God wasn't a religious deity. In fact, the phrase's religious meaning is the sole reason we abandoned our original purely secular motto, E Pluribus Unum (Latin for *Out of many, one*), a phrase that was chosen by a committee of Thomas Jefferson, John Adams, and Benjamin Franklin, and represented the birth, heritage, and history of our nation from 1782 to 1956. Government officials discarded that historic motto and adopted the religious motto In God We Trust to distinguish us from the Soviet Union, which promoted state atheism.

What makes this particular issue so damaging, however, is not that our Supreme Court repeatedly condoned a violation of the Constitution. It's the lengths it went, to do so. In the third case, in 1994, the plaintiffs presented incontrovertible evidence in the form of an independent national survey[37] that the phrase had not lost its religious content and was in fact overwhelmingly perceived as an endorsement of religion, which clearly made it unconstitutional. So when the Supreme Court refused to hear the appeal this time, it not only supressed the explicit factual evidence contained in that survey, it implied that it was unaware of the information it contained, thus making this case particularly egregious and reprehensible. The Court's statement read in part: "We find that a reasonable observer, aware of the purpose, context, and history of the phrase 'In God we trust,' would not consider its use or its reproduction on U.S. currency to be an endorsement of religion" when in fact they knew full well that the exact opposite was true.

Even worse, by couching its statement in terms of "a reasonable observer", the Court artfully implied that it had no way of knowing how people actually perceived the phrase, when in fact it had indisputable evidence containing that specific information. In order to let the previous popular ruling stand, which was by the way devoid of any substantive evidence, the Court chose to ignore hard evidence and artfully imply that it had to rely on conjecture to make its determination.

There's no way to know for sure why these judges felt it necessary to rule in favor of government endorsing religion. But there are at least three possible explanations, especially at the Supreme Court level. The first is that they may have just succumbed to their own emotional need for religion. Not only does the process of selecting these judges ensure they embrace some type of supernatural pretense, but because they are all later in life, that pretense exerts a greater influence on their perspective and behaviors. A second possible explanation is that they may have simply acquiesced to the considerable pressure of religion's popularity, fearing that the Court might lose favor with the nation as a whole if it ruled against such a popular government endorsement. A third possibility is that they may have feared that the moral fabric of society might somehow deteriorate. Even though these are all well-educated judges, just like the public, many remain under the mistaken impression that we derive our values and morality from the imagined notion of a Supreme Being.

But whatever their reasons, such irrational behavior from what is arguably our strongest bastion of objectivity can only be viewed as a harmful capitulation to popular subjectivity. The fact that our most objective institution cannot remain rational in the face of such pressures speaks volumes about how far the rest of us have yet to go in our quest for rationality. Pretending that In God We

Trust has no religious significance is not just disingenuous; it is a gross denial of truth and reality, one that can only be embraced by the friendliest of audiences, and one that would have likely appalled the founding fathers. When Congress creates tax laws that disproportionately benefit religious organizations, or passes laws adopting phrases that invoke a religious deity, it is making laws that regard, concern, touch upon, and relate to religion, which is an act that the First Amendment expressly prohibits. But, again, because we are a predominantly religious country that has yet to recognize the harm that religion causes, we possess little desire to object. Until a majority of citizens recognize that keeping religion out of government affairs is essential to a healthy society, ceremonial deism will remain the go-to oxymoronic catchphrase that judges will use as their quasi-legal rationalization for commingling Church and State, the government will continue to promote irrational behaviors, and the integrity and legitimacy of our legal system will continue to be undermined and degraded.

THE IMMEASURABLE IMPORTANCE OF SEPARATING CHURCH AND STATE

Most everyone thinks that the founding fathers' decision to keep matters of the Church separate from those of the State was a good idea. But few of us give much thought as to why. The elemental reason religion should play no role in government is that religion displaces logic and reason. All the problems the founding fathers witnessed in governments that claimed to be making decisions with divine guidance were but examples of what happens when we dismiss reason on the largest of scales. It results in massive consequences.

The harmful irrational effects of religion in our government can be seen in everything from its decisions to go to war, to the reluctance of lawmakers to endorse policies that benefit society. Sex education, contraception, embryo screening, and what is widely recognized as the gateway to undreamed-of medical breakthroughs, stem cell research, are all good examples. Our proclivity to intermingle Church and State is but another manifestation of our natural desire to attain both comfort and truth where they are exclusive of one another. Until we apprehend that religion only enhances our comfort at the expense of truth, we will continue to suffer the considerable consequences of infusing irrational behaviors into societal affairs.

To the degree we keep Church and State separate, we ensure that group decisions are derived not irrationally from the things that make us feel good, but rationally through logic and reason, the only means we have of purposely accomplishing anything. Even Thomas Jefferson, who was a man of deep religious conviction, spoke strongly in favor of reason over emotion when he wrote: "Question with boldness even the existence of a God; because, if there be one, he must more approve of the homage of reason, than that of blindfolded fear."[38]

Quite often the First Amendment is misconstrued, even intentionally misrepresented, as mandating that our practice of religion be unrestricted. Fortunately, this is not the case. The First Amendment ensures that we can practice religion to our hearts' content as long as others are not forced to participate, which includes financial participation through taxes. It's actually quite straightforward. Because government is funded by tax dollars that are collected from both religious and nonreligious citizens, the First Amendment ensures that we are able to practice religion as long as it does not involve any of those joint funds or force others to participate in religious activities. Though a great many contorted arguments have been made to rationalize violating this

Constitutional mandate, the test to discern such violations is relatively simple. If a religious practice is paid for in whole or in part with government funds (which includes using government owned or maintained properties), because those who are not religious were forced to help pay for it, it violates our Constitution.

ALL RELIGIONS ARE EQUALLY INVALID

Another significant reality we conveniently overlook regarding religion is that no matter how harmful or harmless, no religion is any more valid than any other. Because religion requires that we reject logic and reason and embrace things that we imagine, as knowledge, it necessitates that we jettison the only means we have of determining the validity or veracity of anything. That, in a nutshell, is the problem with religion. It requires that we discard the only means we have of vetting the things we embrace as knowledge and, in so doing, makes possible limitless uncontestable rationalizations for absolutely any behavior. When we ascribe the writings of humans to divine guidance, we elevate those words to the unassailable status of absolute knowledge and thereby create the ultimate sanctuary for our most harmful behaviors.

No matter how different, preposterous, or even harmful someone else's pretense of supernatural knowledge may be, once we reject reality and adopt our own such irrational perspective, we are left with no basis from which to assert that theirs is any less real or important to them. This is why religions that advocate hatred and violence are no less valid than those advocating peace and tolerance. They are all supported by the exact same amount of factual substantiation: absolutely none. Simply put, everyone is dining from the same endless buffet of comfort-filled delusions. When anyone embraces religion, all they have are things that seem valid precisely as much as they desire them to be, a supremely dangerous state of affairs.

RELIGION'S DEPENDENCE ON SELF-DELUSION
Because we are subjective beings by nature, we engage in self-delusion to some degree with everything we experience. And for a great many this becomes manifested in the practice of religion. Despite the fact that we are devoid of certainty regarding the nonphysical or supernatural, religious narratives are rarely conveyed in uncertain terms. When religious leaders speak about what God wants, they don't begin or end their statements with "I think," "I hope," or "allegedly," which is the most anyone can factually assert about such things. Instead, they state things as a matter of fact and erroneously imply, sometimes even claiming outright, that they possess such knowledge. The truth is, however, that no human knows even the slightest bit more than any other about the nonphysical. The world's smartest and most heralded religious leaders know exactly as much about the supernatural as the world's most ignorant atheists: absolutely nothing at all.

What's remarkable is not that religious leaders misrepresent such conjecture as knowledge, but rather why they do. They do it because we, their audience, effectively demand it of them. Only by speaking with an air of certainty are they able to bolster our own delusions of supernatural knowledge, enhance how we feel, and thereby gain a following. In the words of Mark Twain, "Religion consists in a set of things which the average man thinks he believes, and wishes he was certain of."[39] This is why so many people become some kind of evangelist, minister, parson, pastor, preacher, priest, or reverend. It requires absolutely no knowledge and one can become extremely wealthy by simply telling people what they want to hear. By feigning knowledge of the supernatural, these so-called leaders are able to prey on the emotional needs of their audience, people who are more than anxious to reject reality to embrace a story that provides them comfort. In the words of the 20th-century African-American historian, author, and journalist Dr. Carter G. Woodson, "Practically all the incompetents and undesirables who have been barred from other walks of life by race prejudice and economic difficulties have rushed into the ministry for the exploitation of the people."[40] Because those who practice religion remain in constant need of shoring up their precarious source of comfort, there is always considerable demand for those who can pontificate with an air of certainty about what God wants.

For those who have difficulty recognizing or accepting that religion necessitates self-delusion, I would ask that you try answering the following questions truthfully while bearing in mind that the textbook definition of delusion is a false belief held in the face of strong invalidating evidence. In light of the fact that the originating texts for virtually all religions were written during a time when people understood considerably less about the things they experienced and were considerably more susceptible to legends, fables, and folklore, why is it that we are so willing to reject all that we know today to accept what they wrote? Why do we so readily embrace reports of supernatural experiences by others less knowledgeable and disregard the considerable factual evidence to the contrary? Why is it that we regularly congregate to hear someone else speak on a subject that we know no human can have any knowledge? Why is it that all the things we use to support such notions are, without exception, invisible, not repeatable, or otherwise conveniently unavailable for objective scrutiny? Why do we go to such extreme lengths to convince ourselves that there is a God and an afterlife? The simple answer to all these questions is that religion provides us not truth, but comfort at the expense of truth. The fact that we hold our religious freedoms so dear indicates how far we have yet to go before recognizing this most prominent of self-delusions and all the harm it causes.

In words credited to Thomas Edison, "All Bibles are man-made."[41] Because no human is capable of detecting the supernatural, everything that has ever been or will ever be written about any deity or afterlife is necessarily imagined; this is a reality of which we are all, at least subconsciously, aware. This is why, despite religion's popularity and in spite of it being posited as the source of all good, we virtually never hear anyone promoting religion generically. To receive the comfort of any religion, one must embrace it as truth and reality to the exclusion of all others. This is why those who practice religion never perceive themselves as part of the problem. Religion necessitates a self-righteous perspective. To receive its comforts, we must embrace the notion that it isn't our religion or how we practice it that is wrong or harmful, but rather how those other people practice their religion.

Religion requires us to delude ourselves with the notion that people have been able to somehow do that which no human has been demonstrated to do. Even if we don't see ourselves as possessing knowledge of the supernatural, we must embrace the notion that people who came before us were somehow able to not just communicate with the supernatural, but to know with all certainty that such communications were not a delusion of their own making. And therein resides the impossibility. Though we may have *subjective* feelings of certainty about such things, because we have no means by which to become aware or gain knowledge of the nonphysical, we can never be *objectively* certain. To be *objectively* certain requires a rational justification, something that religion cannot provide. To embrace religion, we must subscribe to the notion that human beings of lesser knowledge were able to not just feel, but to know for a fact that the nature and origin of their experience was supernatural, and we must do so in the face of overwhelming evidence to the contrary, exemplifying the quintessential definition of self-delusion.

Again, it demonstrates the entirely irrational nature of religion. If we relied on two-thousand-year-old hearsay that conflicted with everything we know about factual reality in any other aspect of life, we would likely be considered inordinately ignorant, detained for psychological evaluation, or locked up for fraud. Yet we continue to do precisely that when it comes to religion. The irrepressible question being, on exactly what plane of existence does that make any kind of rational sense?

The fact that we embed this practice of self-delusion in our children and leverage their enormous instinctual need for family and social acceptance to ensure they adopt it is what makes it so incredibly difficult to diminish religious conflicts. When children become developed enough to reason for themselves, if they have been inculcated in the practice of religion, they must then choose between what they instinctually determine to be true and real and a pretense that holds the acceptance of family and friends. The somewhat natural result is that their insatiable need for acceptance almost always wins out. Until a majority of society recognizes that religion necessitates self-delusion, our innate need for acceptance will remain the most powerful tool for pressuring others to practice this harmful irrational behavior.

The fact that our need for acceptance is the predominant influence in determining which religion we practice represents one of the most basic self-deceptions required by religion. By far, the thing that most influences which religion we practice is our parents and the particular religion they practice, which in turn is most influenced by the area of the world in which they happen to live. This is why entire families so often practice the same religion, why entire regions of the world are dominated by a single religion, and why most people would likely be practicing a different religion had they been born elsewhere. But such happenstance doesn't exactly accommodate the emotionally satisfying notion of practicing the only religion that represents truth and reality, which is the essential theme of every religion.

The denial of reality required by religion can also be seen in the rationalizations we recite when trying to explain the absolute absence of proof regarding it. One common argument has long held that religion is analogous to our feelings, in that we are also unable to prove how we feel. Fortunately, we have reached a level of awareness that now allows us to demonstrate the fallacy of this argument. Because our feelings are physical in nature, it was just a matter of time before we developed tools that prove they exist. Though there continues to be no proof of God, heaven, or anything supernatural, advances in technology have now made it possible for various sensors and scans to detect and map the physical activities that are our feelings.

PASCAL'S ILL-CONCEIVED WAGER

For more than 350 years now, people have been citing Pascal's Wager as a sound reason for practicing religion. And for more than 350 years now, people have been unequivocally wrong in doing so. For those unfamiliar with Pascal's Wager, it refers to an argument put forth by the 17th-century French philosopher, mathematician, and physicist Blaise Pascal regarding the existence of God. It posits that everyone bets with his or her life that God either does or does not exist. He argued that if God exists the consequences of believing or not believing are infinite, while if God does not exist the consequences are finite. Therefore, a rational person should seek to believe in God. But, even if you ignore the reality that nature affords us no say in the things we believe, and overlook all the unsupported assumptions inherent in Mr. Pascal's argument, there is still a significant fundamental problem with it. He posits only half of the possibilities: that one would experience infinite good from religious adherence or infinite harm from religious disobedience. In reality, because we possess absolutely no information regarding the supernatural, it is equally possible and likely that we would experience the exact opposite: infinite harm from religious adherence and infinite good from religious disobedience.

The inherent deception of Pascal's Wager is that it proffers only one side of an imagined premise. Because we have yet to recognize that religion is entirely imagined, like the athletes who only point to the sky when they catch the ball, Pascal only included the possibilities that coincided with a comforting version of the supernatural. But in fact, anytime we use an entirely imagined premise in our decision making, if our thinking is to remain rational, we must give equal weight to the exact opposite imaginary possibilities, which is something Pascal's Wager fails to do. Accordingly, Pascal's Wager posits not what a rational person would do, but rather what an irrational person would do, which dismantles his entire argument.

RELIGION – SPIRITUAL SNAKE OIL FOR AILING VALUES AND MORALS

As briefly touched on earlier, the most common misconception regarding religion is that of it improving our behaviors. This notion serves as the basic premise of and justification for all religions, as well as the conflicts they generate. Consequently, if there is a single most important realization to be garnered from this book, it is that, in spite of all we've been taught and conditioned to think, religious people do not behave better than those who are not religious, a fact that dispels the only pseudo-pragmatic reason for practicing religion. And the world is saturated with empirical data that unequivocally demonstrates this ubiquitous reality, should we make even the slightest effort to seek it out.

Though it may come as a somewhat disconcerting revelation to those who are religious, the evidence is overwhelming that humanity would exhibit just as many good behaviors, if not more, without religion. Again, take a moment to look at the larger picture and consider the obvious. After thousands of years and the incalculable experiences of billions upon billions of people, there exists absolutely no credible data of any type that even remotely suggests religion does what it is purported to do: improve behavior. This is why when we witness someone doing something good, we don't automatically think to ourselves, "That person must be religious." We know, at least subconsciously, that nonreligious people are just as likely to do good deeds. It's just that, because this false narrative has been so deeply seated in our thinking since the time we were little, we mistakenly, and oftentimes conveniently, view the good things people do in the name of religion, as being caused by religion.

If there were even the slightest bit of factual information supporting the notion that religion makes us better people, it would no doubt have surfaced by now. Any such causal relationship would have become manifest in objective data that religious people would prominently display to support their practice. At the very least, those trying to convert the nonreligious would certainly use such data in support of their cause. But in fact, conspicuously absent from all the religions of the world is even the slightest factual evidence that it makes us better human beings, which should be a giant red flag to anyone seeking the truth about how religion actually affects our behavior.

Even though those who are religious feel increasingly pressured to defend their practice and the mining of data has emerged as one of our most prolific and lucrative industries, no one has statistically demonstrated that religion in any way improves behavior, much less which particular religions are most effective at doing so. If religion actually improved behavior, it only stands to reason that at least some of us, if not all of us, would want to know which religions were most effective at doing so. The same instinctual concerns that have us scrutinizing schools over their ability to teach our children would have us scrutinizing religions even more, to determine which ones instilled the best values and morals. But when it comes to seeking factual information about the efficacy of religion, as the saying goes, the silence is deafening.

Because our only concern with religion is not how it affects our behavior, but rather how it makes us feel, such functional data is not wanted or needed, nor will it ever be, by those who practice religion. This is why even well-intended attempts to rationally discuss religion invariably go nowhere. Because religion is by its very nature entirely irrational, all we can factually discuss regarding it is how it makes us feel. This is why even certifiable geniuses can sound less than intelligent when trying to rationalize their religious convictions: there are no rational explanations. In the words of our 15th President, James Buchanan, "I have seldom met an intelligent person whose views were not narrowed and distorted by religion."[42]

The fact that religion does not improve behavior is a ubiquitous reality that is easily recognized by those who are not religious. But for those who are religious, the notion that religion provides benefit to society is the closest thing they have to a rational explanation for engaging in it. It's their only recourse when explaining, defending, or otherwise justifying religion, which makes it somewhat indispensable to their frame of mind. This is why when someone does harm in the name of a particular religion, others who practice that religion feel compelled to say that the person wasn't practicing "true" Christianity, Islam, Hinduism, or whatever the religion happens to be, or that the person wasn't interpreting its originating text correctly. But in fact, there is no such thing as a correct practice or interpretation of any religion. Even if we accept a single book as being the authority on a particular religion, because religion must be entirely imagined, by nature, there are literally as many interpretations of that book as there are people who read it, and none are any more valid or correct than any other.

We also often mistake, or at least conveniently confuse, religious contributions as charitable contributions. Though the two often overlap, they are performed for very different reasons. When we make either type of contribution, we do so for the same basic reason we exhibit all the rest of our social behaviors: to enhance our acceptance. The noteworthy difference is that we make religious contributions to seek the acceptance of those who share our delusion of supernatural knowledge, those who can shore up our precarious source of comfort.

Several studies have shown that those who practice religion volunteer more and give more than those who are not religious. The illusion being that religion makes them more charitable. What those studies failed to consider is that when people participate regularly in any type of organization or group, they contribute more to it, to ensure their acceptance with that particular group of people. It's akin to paying dues to receive the benefits of a club. The more you enjoy what the club provides, the more you're willing to pay for the experience. In the case of religion, it enables us to feel good by affirming our most significant delusion. This is how the Catholic Church has become one of the wealthiest organizations on the face of the Earth. Because religion only enhances how we feel to the extent we become convinced we have knowledge of the supernatural, those who have become addicted to its tenuous comfort will pay handsomely to have the Church dispense "knowledge" of the unknowable. The Church, on the other hand, has learned that by presenting itself as a source of supernatural knowledge, it can extract enormous amounts of money from that same group of people. This is why religions preach so much guilt. It amplifies the demand for the fallacious services they provide. In the words of the late 18th/early 19th-century French military and political leader Napoleon Bonaparte, "I am surrounded by priests who repeat incessantly that their kingdom is not of this world, and yet they lay their hands on everything they can get."[43]

Those studies also fail to mention that a significant portion of the religious volunteer work is directed at benefiting the Church and that a lot of religious contributions go toward purchasing church assets. And if you think that doesn't amount to much, I would point out that it is the self-serving nature of religious donations that has made the Catholic Church so incredibly wealthy, a reality that epitomizes the considerable distinction between *religious* deeds and *charitable* deeds. Because religious donations are more about shoring up our own precarious source of comfort than helping others, we care more about making them than we do about how and where that money gets spent, which is precisely what enables the Church to usurp a great deal of them.

When it comes to religious donations, we conveniently overlook the fact that the definition of charitable is not doing that which engorges the coffers of the Church, but rather benefiting the indigent, ill, or helpless. And if you find yourself questioning the sincerity or legitimacy of that statement, I would ask that you try to imagine how much charitable good could be done with the billions upon billions of dollars the Catholic Church has amassed in businesses, prime real estate, priceless art, gold, cash, and investments. I would also ask that you think about where all that money comes from. Whether it's as mainstream as the Catholic Church or as commercial as TV evangelism, think about all the poor people who, with what little hope and money they have, are guilted into giving to such organizations. No, in those instances where religious donations exceed nonreligious donations, it doesn't signify that religion improves our behavior; it signifies that religious organizations are more willing to provide a fallacious service to take advantage of those who are most in need, emotionally and financially.

WHAT ACTUALLY SHAPES OUR VALUES AND MORALITY

The thing that impels our social behaviors is not any kind of pretend knowledge about the supernatural. It is our strong instinctual need for acceptance. Our values and morality are manifestations of the degree to which our innate desire for acceptance influences our behavior. And because that desire is genetically driven, it means that, once again, we have it backwards. Our religions do not shape our values and morals; our instinctually determined values and morals served to shape our religions.

Because our need for acceptance arrived on the scene long before we developed the conscious ability to imagine any religion, it served as a kind of template around which we created our many religions. This is why many religious teachings are thought to have originated with philosophers such as Aristotle, Plato, and Confucius, who lived centuries earlier. The innate need they reflect has existed for untold millennia. It's why we still identify with much of what is written in religious texts. Those documents represent early attempts to codify social behaviors. In those instances where the authors got it right and encouraged behaviors that actually benefit society, their words remain valid and continue to resonate. But because those texts were written during a time when people understood a lot less about which behaviors were best for society, they often got it wrong, which is why we are continually having to change how we interpret them. This is one of the fundamental problems with any religion. Because they require that their originating text be embraced as the word of God, as absolute knowledge, they prohibit followers from embracing new behaviors that are shown to be more beneficial, as we become more aware.

The fact that our social behaviors are not consciously initiated, but rather instinctually impelled, has been demonstrated in the multitude of studies showing that we experience significantly higher levels of stress when simply in the presence of another human being. That additional pressure is our genetic instructions urging us to behave in a way that facilitates our acceptance. Feelings such as guilt, shame, pride, disgrace, embarrassment, and humiliation represent the physiological leverage by which our genetic instructions impel us to behave in a socially acceptable manner. This is what makes blame and peer pressure such powerful tools of manipulation and why being shunned is so incredibly difficult to endure. When rejected by the group, our genetic instructions trigger extraordinarily powerful chemical responses to effect behaviors that will regain our acceptance.

THE PROBLEM WITH ATHEISTS IS THEY PRESENT NO PROBLEM

Perhaps the most prominent example of religion's permeating harm can be seen in how religious people feel about atheists. Virtually every study, poll, and survey ever conducted on the subject has shown that atheists are the most despised minority. And if one is religious, that probably makes perfect sense, for fundamental to religion is the false notion that it provides our values and morals. But whether you are religious or not, have you ever stopped to question what it is about atheists that make them so reviled? It's not that they might be headed toward eternal damnation, for that would evoke sympathy, compassion, or perhaps empathy, not hatred. And if your answer has anything to do with behavior, have you ever asked yourself where you got the notion that atheists behave worse than religious people? If you were able to answer these two questions honestly you now realize that there is no rational basis from which to feel even the slightest misgivings about atheists. No matter how old you are or what path you have traveled, you have not seen even a single credible study that shows atheists behave worse or are any less trustworthy than those who practice religion, because no such study exists. As much as some would like to believe that their disdain for atheists has a sound factual basis, there is not the slightest scintilla of factual data or evidence to support such a notion. Unfortunately, that reality scarcely inconveniences those who practice religion. Because religion provides a kind of blanket rationalization for even our most deplorable feelings, the basic ubiquitous fact that atheists do not behave worse is of no consequence to those who feel the need to despise them.

A rather revealing clue as to why religious people loathe atheists can be found in the fact that atheists have no discernible features or characteristics that would distinguish them in a crowd. Given the fact that they do not behave worse and cannot be singled out by their appearance, what is it about atheists that religious people so detest? The answer is actually quite simple, and easy to see if you don't happen to be burdened with such feelings and the constant need to rationalize them. Atheists are subjected to more hatred, bigotry, and prejudice than any other minority for one reason and one reason only: they represent a perspective that fundamentally undermines the tenuous comfort that religion provides.

Because religion cannot be explained or defended with factual reality, we subconsciously know that the comfort it provides is precarious, at best. And because atheists embrace the very realities that religious people must constantly dodge and deny, they are unconsciously perceived as a threat to that comfort. This is why those who are religious don't ever have to meet an atheist to detest them. It's not the person or anything they do that makes them so unnerving; it's that they embrace the realities that cast doubt on religion. This is why atheists remain a glaring exception to the increased social tolerance afforded minorities over the last several decades. In the polite words of Penny Edgell, an associate sociology professor and lead researcher in a University of Minnesota study on atheists[44], "It seems most Americans believe that diversity is fine, as long as everyone shares a common 'core' of values that make them trustworthy — and in America, that 'core' has historically been religious." This is but one of the many ways that religion, and the false notion that it provides us our values and morality, spawns hatred and prejudice that estranges a great many good and decent people.

PULLING BACK THE CURTAIN ON HOW RELIGION ACTUALLY AFFECTS OUR BEHAVIOR

In the words of the early 19th-century English poet George Gordon Byron, better known as Lord Byron, "Of religion I know nothing – at least, in its favor."[45] The only consistent and notable effect religion has on our behavior is that of impeding rational thought and providing spurious rationalizations for acting on what we feel. Consequently, discomforting as it may be for those who are religious, religion actually imparts a detrimental effect on behavior. When we ascribe any behavior, good or bad, to religion, we are imagining an explanation for something we do not understand, an act that always has consequences. Though religion enables us to feel better in the here and now, history demonstrates that no behavior extracts a higher price for doing so, making it our most harmful nearsighted behavior. Human life is never about following a religion, but rather always about following our genetic directives to attain the greatest benefit, an endeavor best served through a mixture of rational individual and social behaviors. This is why, religious or not, all people possess the same innate desire to be treated equally, with dignity and respect. Such behaviors facilitate a peaceful and prosperous coexistence, the need for which is deeply embedded in our genetic priorities.

The only difference between those who practice religion and those who do not is an intrinsically irrational religious conviction. All human behaviors originate from our common instinctual needs. But because religion requires an irrational perspective, it imparts an additional source of conflict, both internally and socially, which has a permeating negative effect on behavior. In the book *The Psychology of Religion*, the authors Bernard Spilka, Ralph W. Hood Jr., and Richard Gorsuch state that most studies show conventional religion is not an effective force for moral behavior or against criminal activity[46]. They also cite studies showing a higher rate of religious affiliation among criminals and juvenile delinquents, a finding substantiated by data gathered from more than 173,000 prisoners by the U.S. Department of Justice, Federal Bureau of Prisons[47].

A nationwide study of 16,000 public and nonpublic high school seniors that was commissioned by the National Catholic Educational Association and funded in part by the National Institute on Drug Abuse[48] revealed that even though Catholic schools expel problem students who later end up in public schools, Catholic high school students were more likely to use alcohol, cocaine, marijuana, and steal, than those in public schools. Another study, titled "The Negative Association between Religiousness and Children's Altruism across the World"[49], which was conducted across six countries and focused on children between the ages of 5 and 12, found that religion negatively influences a child's altruism. Further, when it comes to abortions, 32% of Protestant women and 29% of Catholic women reported having them, compared to only 22% of women who professed no religious affiliation[50]. And while religious people revile atheists the most, they are by no means alone. In a 2009 meta-analysis of 55 independent studies containing more than 20,000 participants[51], the authors found that there was a correlation between religion and racism. The more devout a person was in their practice of religion, the more they tended to harbor prejudiced views of other races. All of which makes perfect sense when you consider the fact that religion requires an irrational mindset that can rationalize absolutely any feeling, thought, or behavior. Because religion by its very nature precludes logic and reason, it facilitates the very behaviors it is supposed to prevent. When we embrace religion, we do so not because of but rather in spite of its effects on our behavior, for the comfort it provides.

In essence, those who are not religious are able to maintain a somewhat higher degree of rationality throughout the course of their lives, which naturally gets reflected in their behaviors. Unlike religious people, nonreligious people possess no blanket rationalization for their harmful behaviors. They don't set up schools, television programs, and radio broadcasts to inculcate people in irrational thinking and then extract money from them once they've become habituated to the practice. Unlike religious people, nonreligious people feel no need to permeate the highest levels of business and government with irrational thinking. They harbor no pretense of supernatural knowledge that would compel them to shun intellectual thought or inquiry. Conspicuously absent from the behaviors of the nonreligious is the incessant need to reject logic and reason and pressure others to do the same. Indoctrinating our children with a pretense of supernatural knowledge does more than just diminish their capacity to reason. It unnecessarily burdens them with an increasingly distorted and conflicted perspective, something that subsequently pervades every aspect of their lives.

THE MANY WAYS RELIGION GENERATES HARM

The harm of religion has been present since its inception. In the words of the Roman poet and philosopher Titus Lucretius Carus, who died some 50 years before Jesus was born, "All religions are equally sublime to the ignorant, useful to the politician, and ridiculous to the philosopher."[52] The Roman Stoic philosopher and statesman Lucius Annaeus Seneca, who lived about 100 years after Lucretius, echoed his sentiments: "Religion is regarded by the common people as true, by the wise as false, and by rulers as useful."[53] And the 19th-century French writer Marie-Henri Beyle, better known by his pen name of Stendhal, wrote: "All religions are founded on the fear of the many and the cleverness of the few."[54]

The most overt harm of religion is without question the large-scale conflicts that it generates. Again, because survival is our ultimate instinctual priority, nothing produces more internal discomfort than our apprehension of death. And because the human imagination serves to create things that improve how we feel, a pretense of supernatural knowledge becomes the perfect vehicle for escaping that greatest of all discomforts. The problem is that we must necessarily leave behind truth and reality to receive that comfort, an act that ensures conflict. This is why people who are exceedingly religious are often avoided and ostracized. Their perspective becomes so distorted that they become dissociated from rational society. Envision the problems it would create if a child insisted that their behaviors were being prompted by an imaginary friend who was more important than any adult. Now multiply those effects by several orders of magnitude and you begin to get some idea of how harmful it can be when adults do it.

One of the more permeating harms that religion inflicts is its intrinsic need to obstruct learning. Beyond the fact that religion enables us to rationalize even our most abhorrent behaviors, once we fill in what we do not know with things that we imagine and embrace them as knowledge, not only do we stop looking for truth, we feel the need to reject it when it eventually emerges, a propensity that significantly impedes the growth of human understanding. It's impossible to know just how much further the entire world would be along the ever-steepening curve of human awareness if so many truths had not been considered heresy and suppressed by the Church hundreds of years ago. One can only imagine what groundbreaking discoveries we might now be making if leading thinkers such as da Vinci, Copernicus, and Galileo had not been condemned and prohibited from teaching their discoveries all those generations ago.

Though we like to think of such irrational behaviors as a thing of the past, sadly, they are not. You only have to look at the Church's current position on embryo screening or stem cell research to see how even greater strides are being stifled today. Not only is religion slowing the development of lifesaving advancements in medicine, but by opposing the testing of embryos, it is inhibiting the for certain prevention of deadly diseases such as cystic fibrosis, Tay-Sachs disease, muscular dystrophy, sickle-cell disease, hemophilia, Huntington's disease, early onset Alzheimer's disease, colon cancer, breast cancer, and a host of other incurable conditions.

Because religious freedom is nothing more than the freedom to seek psychological comfort at the expense of reality, it is quite literally the freedom to think and act irrationally at the expense of safe peaceful coexistence. If left unchecked, religious freedom would plunge any society into anarchy. This is why our courts must constantly weigh our religious rights and freedoms against all our other rights and freedoms. They must continually determine how much irrational behavior society can tolerate to facilitate this popular psychological shortcut to comfort. This is why courts have ruled that people can opt out of having their children vaccinated, for religious reasons, but have ruled against the exact same argument regarding more imminent threats to life. No matter how much unwarranted comfort religion may provide, there is a limit to how much harm we are willing to accept to receive that comfort. And for most people, fortunately, that limit is well short of sacrificing human life.

To get some idea of just how attached we are to this comforting pretense of supernatural knowledge, consider the fact that we could end all the religious conflicts around the world within the span of a single generation if everyone taught their children one very simple and incontrovertible truth: No one has any knowledge of God or any kind of afterlife; all we have is our hopes and desires. Now, if you can envision the infinitesimally small likelihood of all parents in all parts of the world actually imparting that one unequivocal truth to their children, you begin to get some idea of just how emotionally dependent mankind still is on this most prominent of self-delusions. The significance of religion does not lie in the knowledge of God's existence; it lies in how we deal with the complete absence thereof.

Hoping and knowing are worlds apart when it comes to the comfort they provide, which by nature makes them worlds apart in the devastation they can cause. It's hard to kill someone for merely *hoping* that something is true. But once we convince ourselves that we *know* what God wants, human life can become trivial in the face of that ultimate pretense. In the immortal words of Mark Twain, "It ain't what you don't know that gets you into trouble. It's what you know for sure that just ain't so."[55] But religion only provides its comfort if and to the extent we embrace what we have imagined, as knowledge, with a delusional certainty that precludes reason.

Once we begin relying on religion to improve how we feel, much like the drug addict who needs to keep using, we must maintain that delusion of knowledge to sustain our comfort. Without that self-induced pretense, religion becomes just another story in a book, no different than tales of mermaids, unicorns, or leprechauns. This is what makes religion so enduring and so dangerous. Like any addictive drug, it hijacks our primal form of guidance and entraps its practitioners in a powerful dependency. As the 17th-century French philosopher and writer Pierre Bayle once wrote, "In matters of religion, it is very easy to deceive a man, and very hard to undeceive him."[56]

To get some idea of the price that humanity pays to receive comfort from religion, it helps to step back and look at the bigger picture. Globally, there is a strong correlation between a lack of religion and a better life. It's not some kind of perpetual worldwide coincidence that countries such as Japan, Sweden, Denmark, Norway, Australia, Netherlands, New Zealand, Austria, Belgium, Canada, Switzerland, Iceland, and Finland are some of the least religious societies on Earth and also consistently ranked as the happiest and in the top twenty for social and economic development, by the United Nations Human Development Report, a group that uses life expectancy, educational attainment, per capita income, and gender equality among their criteria. It reflects the fundamental correlation that exists between our degree of rationality and the effectiveness with which we conduct our lives. Because our degree of rationality is unconsciously established at an early age, it naturally gets passed down from one generation to the next, leaving entire nations to continually reap the benefits or suffer the consequences thereof. The all-important point being, we no longer have to guess at the effects of religion. We have an entire world of empirical data that categorically demonstrates we do not need a pretense of supernatural knowledge to do good things, a somewhat obvious reality for those who have not been conditioned to ignore and reject it.

The very nature of religion is such that it precludes us from seeing the harm in our own practice. Even if we acknowledge that religion has to be imagined and only makes us feel better, we still see it as a good thing. Our tendency is to think how can something that inspires so much good be harmful? Well, the short and simple answer is that the more we become emotionally invested in any pretense or delusion, the more we distort both our perspective and our behaviors, to sustain the comfort it provides.

Setting aside all the wars that have been waged in the name of religion, a prominent example of how even a mainstream religion can cause unspeakable harm can be seen in the numerous child molestations perpetrated by leaders of the Catholic Church. Virtually everyone has heard about them and thought how terrible it was that such trusted leaders could take advantage of those innocent children. But noteworthy and appalling as those molestations were, they did not constitute the most harmful effects. Much more insidious and devastating was the abandonment and helplessness those children felt when they wanted to go to their parents. Inconceivable as it may be, common in the testimony of the victims was the fear that if they reported the abuse, their parents would side with the Church. Now we'd all like to think that those poor children just didn't understand the depth of a parent's love for a child, that they were surely wrong in their assessment of the situation. But as it turns out, those children had it exactly right. Some did in fact report the abuse only to be called liars and physically disciplined for suggesting that these pious men of God could do such a thing.

What's so incredibly important to understand is how and why this situation came to exist. It wasn't that these parents were bad people or didn't love their children. Just like everyone else who practices religion, these parents had the best of intentions. The problem was that they had become emotionally invested in religion. They had come to rely so much on this delusional source of comfort that they were willing to put the safety and wellbeing of their own children at unconscionable risk, to sustain it. They wanted so much to believe that these people who had presented themselves as righteous and devout leaders had knowledge of the supernatural, that they could no longer even consider the reality of them being just ordinary people and capable of such acts. This is how religion imparts harm to every person who practices it. It necessitates a distortion of reality that permeates every aspect of our thoughts and behaviors. Just like everyone else who deludes themselves into thinking they have knowledge of the supernatural, these parents convinced themselves that they were doing the right thing. Because they had been instilled with the mistaken notion that religion provides our values and morals, they didn't recognize that even such well-intentioned pretenses prompt a distortion of reality that can cause indescribable harm.

The next time you find yourself thinking that your religious involvement isn't harmful, try to remember how these children suffered irreparable harm because of their parents' well-meaning religious convictions. Try to remember that their parents were not part of any radical group or cult; they were merely average people seeking what they thought would be best for their children from a mainstream religion. Try to be mindful that only by becoming irrational and revering the Church and its authorities to the exclusion of truth and reality can we embrace its pretense and become susceptible to committing such harms. Only to the extent we recognize how this tragedy was made possible and avoid such delusional pretenses ourselves will our children feel safe in approaching us with truth when they desperately need to. In the words of the American theoretical physicist and Nobel laureate Steven Weinberg, "With or without religion you would have good people doing good things and evil people doing evil things. But for good people to do evil things, that takes religion."[57]

HOW RELIGION UNDERMINES THE PRECIOUS NATURE OF LIFE

A common notion among those who practice religion is that without it life would have no meaning (i.e., without religion there would be nothing to live for). But in reality, quite the opposite is true. We can and often do delude ourselves into thinking that something is more significant than it is. This is why we create games of pretend when we're little. They enable us to imagine that our childish actions have grownup relevance. But the actual importance of anything is not determined by our conscious imaginings. It is naturally and necessarily determined by our unconscious instinctual priorities. For anyone to infer or imply that to live life without religion is to live life without meaning is to effectively say that life has no value unless we imagine some kind of conscious explanation for it, which simply isn't the case. Because survival is dependent on discerning reality, by nature, the simple quality of being real gives our experiences more depth, meaning, and value than anything we can consciously conceive.

Not only does such imagined importance not give life meaning, it actually detracts from it. When we delude ourselves into thinking we have knowledge of an afterlife, it necessarily diminishes the precious nature of life in the present; hence the unrivaled willingness of religious people around the world and throughout history to take life. It's somewhat analogous to the mindset of a counterfeiter. By creating an endless supply, money begins to lose its value. By pretending that life doesn't end, but rather continues forever and even gets better after we die, the only effect it can possibly have is to diminish how we perceive it in the here and now. This is how radical religions, cults, and terrorist groups convince people to take human life. They diminish the significance of life here on Earth by furthering the delusion of a better life after death.

What's important to recognize is that it isn't just the radical fringe elements of religion that devalue life. A pretense of life after death is intrinsic to religion in general, which means that even mainstream religions unconsciously devalue how we perceive life in the present. One of the most fundamental and universal laws of nature holds that the more limited something is, the more precious it becomes. By simply accepting the fact that we have no knowledge of anything beyond our existing life, by nature, every moment becomes dearer. Perhaps Thomas Paine expressed it best when he wrote "Tis dearness only that gives everything its value."[58]

When someone dies, we often find ourselves wishing we had done things a little differently, perhaps spent a little more time with them or treated them a little better. The reason we feel this way is that it is our human nature to suppress the reality of life's brevity, which naturally manifests in behaviors we look back on and regret when it's over. This realization is perhaps nowhere more eloquently reflected than in the following words, which are widely credited to the late 18th/early 19th-century French-born Quaker missionary Stephen Grellet: "I expect to pass through this world but once. Any good thing therefore that I can do, or any kindness that I can show to any fellow creature, let me do it now. Let me not defer or neglect it, for I shall not pass this way again."[59] Whenever we use psychological shortcuts, such as religion, to escape life's harsher moments, we unwittingly blunt the extraordinary pleasure of its exquisite moments. In the ageless words of American poet Emily Dickinson, "That it will never come again is what makes life so sweet."[60]

OUR UNWITTING COMPLICITY IN RELIGIOUS CONFLICTS THE WORLD OVER

If you are religious, when you came across things in this text that reflected poorly on religion, you likely brushed them off as not pertaining to you and your practice, without really thinking about it. But global discord is not the product of any particular religion. It is the result of irrational thinking, which is intrinsic to all religions. Every person who practices religion must convince them self that their own unique imaginings are real and that everyone else's are not. The same irrationality that causes others to take life is a latent component of even the most passive religious practices. It just hasn't yet encountered the nature and level of discomfort required to produce such extreme behaviors. Religious conflicts and terrorism will not end until we confront the root cause within ourselves, until we too are willing to cease the irrational practice of procuring our comfort at the expense of truth and reality.

The practice of religion epitomizes the harm that can result when we dismiss the need for objective certainty and instead allow ourselves to act on subjective certainty. By nature, everyone wants to feel good. We just have to guard against taking such psychological shortcuts. When we fail to require some type of repeatable experience or observable proof as the measure by which we determine our certainty, our imagination can fabricate whatever we need to rationalize whatever we do. Austrian-born Adolf Hitler, a self-proclaimed catholic and dictator of Nazi Germany, once said "I believe that I am acting in accordance with the will of the Almighty Creator: by defending myself against the Jew, I am fighting for the work of the Lord."[61] Perhaps even more poignant, Hitler also said, "I have followed [the Catholic Church] in giving our party program the character of unalterable finality, like the Creed"[62] and "The Church has realized that anything and everything can be built up on a document of that sort, no matter how contradictory or irreconcilable with it. The faithful will swallow it whole, so long as logical reasoning is never allowed to be brought to bear on it."[62] In 1936, Hitler told Bishop Berning of Osnabruch, "I am only doing what the Church has done for fifteen hundred years, only more effectively."[63] Given that religion is the only widely accepted practice capable of rationalizing absolutely any behavior, it should come as no surprise that Nazi Germany, the country that started World War II and perpetrated the Holocaust, was the most religious in Europe.

A SIGNIFICANT INTERIM MORAL QUESTION

Given that religion should not be banned or prohibited, that it should dissolve naturally as a result of our increasing awareness, there remains the question of its practice by our children. Is it morally right, or even acceptable, to implant such irrationality in our children? We have evolved to the point where we no longer allow parents to abuse their children physically. Yet when it comes to indoctrinating our children with a distorted perspective, we still allow, even encourage, parents to impose such permanent debilitating impediments on their children, for no better reason than the near-term comfort it provides. Like our Pledge of Allegiance, religion doesn't teach a child *how* to think, it teaches them *what* to think, which invariably leads to conflict. As Spanish-born Mexican filmmaker Luis Bunuel put it, "God and Country make an unbeatable team; they break all records for oppression and bloodshed."[64] Rather than programming our children in the religious dogmas of less knowledgeable past generations, shouldn't we teach them how to think for themselves so they can benefit from their natural progression in awareness? Hasn't history provided us enough empirical data to demonstrate what happens when we don't?

12

The Costly Divisive Effects of Not Understanding Human Behavior

It's relatively easy to recognize that the rate at which human beings are acquiring knowledge is growing by leaps and bounds. What isn't quite so obvious is that, because it takes time for knowledge to fully permeate our consciousness, we often feel more aware than we actually are. For instance, though we know we are a species of animal, we have yet to think of ourselves as such. This is why dictionaries still contain definitions for the word animal that exclude humans. We still misperceive ourselves as being somehow exempt from the many traits and qualities that make us a species of animal, a misstep that greatly impedes our understanding of human behavior.

The fact that we view our behaviors not as purposeful instinctual efforts to obtain benefit, but rather as arbitrary conscious choices, makes it difficult to recognize and agree on solutions to societal problems. Think how much easier it would be to reach a consensus on how to fix a problem if everyone understood that the laws of nature are just as absolute and definite as the laws of physics, and that changing an unwanted behavior is as simple and certain as making it no longer the most beneficial.

This fundamental lack of awareness regarding human behavior is how and why our different political factions have come to exist. Because we have yet to grasp how human behaviors are instinctually derived, we each invariably form our own somewhat mistaken ideas about what it will take to solve societal problems. And because we naturally gravitate toward and affiliate with those of similar thinking, it was not just natural, but inevitable, that we would come to form coalitions around our two largest such misconceptions.

One family of flawed thinking centers on our inability to recognize the essential role that incentive plays in determining our behaviors. It's not just an unfortunate accident that the ranks of those who need government assistance are growing larger at an alarming rate[65, 66]; it is the naturally certain outcome of the policies we have put in place. Because we have yet to apprehend that self-benefit is the sole impetus for all our behaviors, we continue to enact policies that actually discourage people from becoming self-sufficient.

The other family of flawed thinking centers on our inability to recognize what impels our social behaviors. Rather than seeing them as genetically prompted events intended to procure the pragmatic benefits of living and working together, we still see them as selfless acts inspired by a consciously imagined supernatural being. Again, it's not any kind of statistical aberration or mistake that people who practice religion behave somewhat worse than people who do not. [44, 46, 47, 48, 49, 50, 51]. To the degree we adopt and become accustomed to such irrational thinking, it subtly permeates and distorts every aspect of our lives. The fact that three out of four Americans profess a belief in such things as ghosts, witches, and communicating with the dead[67], and only one in five profess a belief in Darwin's theory of evolution[68], is symptomatic of a country that endorses irrationality to the exclusion of truth, reality, logic, and reason.

Because these are our two most prominent misperceptions regarding human behavior, they have become the principal coalescing agents for our two largest political parties, commonly known as the left and the right, liberals and conservatives, or Democrats and Republicans. To the degree we fail to recognize that our actions are prompted solely by the prospect of benefit, we are more likely to support government policies that diminish incentive by taking money from some people and giving it to others, which makes us more likely to identify with and assimilate into the former group. To the degree we fail to recognize that the concern we show for others is not inspired by the conscious notion of a supernatural being, but rather impelled by our instinctual need for acceptance, we are more likely to identify with and assimilate into the latter group.

The fact that there is considerable overlap in these misperceptions is why almost no one aligns entirely with either party. The fact that each group largely has right what the other has wrong is why each can so readily see the flaws in the other's thinking but not in their own. This is the essence of why politics are somewhat impervious to logic and reason, why it evokes vitriolic animosity, and why it results in intransigent positions. At its core are notions of human behavior that are largely invalid and therefore indefensible, a condition that causes our government to grow ever more inefficient, inept, and quarrelsome while the two largest groups of citizens contentiously argue over ineffective fixes.

The all-important point being, these two massive segments of our population remain in perpetual conflict not because one is right and the other is wrong, not because one apprehends reality and the other doesn't, but because each holds a different partially flawed understanding of human behavior. Because virtually everyone has it partially right and partially wrong, we have naturally banded together with those who possess a similar set of right and wrong perceptions, in a futile battle to have one of these two critically flawed lines of thinking succeed. Imagine how much more productive, self-sufficient, rational, and cohesive society would be if everyone clearly understood that you cannot seize the fruits of one's labors without diminishing the desire to work and produce, and you cannot elevate values or morality by having people embrace an irrational pretense of supernatural knowledge.

No matter the problem or conflict, the solution is always an increase in awareness. Until we begin to grasp that all our behaviors, conscious or otherwise, are the result of our genetic instructions interacting with an entirely physical environment for the sole purpose of effecting our survival, we will suffer the consequences of our misperceptions and the conflicting rationalizations they invariably occasion.

13

Our Growing Awareness

Our awareness represents the degree to which we understand the truths that make up our human experience, the extent to which we perceive things as they actually are. The greatest limitation we face in acquiring our awareness is the amount of time we have to do so. We must garner whatever knowledge we can in the span of a single lifetime.

Unlike our instincts, our conscious knowledge, as well as its influence on our behaviors, does not get passed down through genetic instruction. Because our conscious capabilities effectively begin at birth and build upon themselves, our knowledge starts at zero and increases over the course of our lives. It's what determines how far our behaviors transition from those of nature, to those of nurture, from those pursuing essential immediate benefits, to those seeking ever greater and more complex benefits. We assimilate as many new realizations as possible into our picture of reality, in the time we have.

The fact that each generation must begin anew and develop its conscious knowledge is what makes our ability to communicate so fundamentally important. By passing on what we learn, each new generation is able to travel further down the path of awareness. This is what enables humans to advance so much faster than any other life form. We have come to possess both the ability and innate desire to pass on what we learn. This is why it feels good to teach, and why those who possess the capability feel a responsibility, nature impels it. In the words of Isaac Newton, "If I have seen further, it is by standing on the shoulders of giants."[69]

But a rapidly expanding awareness doesn't happen without growing pains. Without question the largest problem a growing awareness poses for any society is that it does not occur uniformly across all walks of life. Because those in the upper levels of society have greater access to education and knowledge, that segment of the population commonly becomes more aware faster, an effect that compounds over time. Historians have noted that most civilizations throughout antiquity have collapsed after only a couple of hundred years. But they have reached no consensus as to why. The human quality at the center of this ageless phenomenon is our rapidly growing awareness. Regardless of a society's location, its system of government, or its available natural resources, those with the most understanding will naturally learn to take greater advantage of the rules, to the detriment of everyone else. Only as the masses become aware of this natural phenomenon will we begin to sufficiently monitor and update the rules, to preclude it from happening.

A broad view of America's vital statistics reveals a country in the latter stages of this somewhat natural progression. Bear in mind that competition is the essential component of nature that serves to keep life healthy. For any society to remain healthy it must ensure fair competition, something that requires the rules to be constantly updated, to keep pace with human awareness. Unfortunately, that hasn't happened in this country. Between 1913 and 1971, some 58 years, we updated our Constitution eleven times, with Amendments 16 through 26. But in the 47 years since, even though we've become more aware at a faster rate, we have enacted only one relatively inconsequential amendment defining when congressional pay raises go into effect. It's not that our awareness has suddenly stopped growing or that we've arrived at the perfect Constitution. It's that those in power have gotten very good at exploiting the system we have, and they don't want changes that would diminish their considerable advantage. By not updating the rules by which they themselves operate, our political representatives have been able to stave off the transparency that is increasingly needed to hold them accountable. The somewhat inevitable effect being, they have increasingly violated the Constitution, committed felony crimes, destroyed evidence, and avoided prosecution, all by working together behind the scenes.

It's safe to say that political corruption has been around since the first politician. But it hasn't always been such a dominant force. Somewhere in the late 1960's the influence of special interests began to exceed that of citizens. Political exploitation became sophisticated and extensive enough to take precedence over societal concerns in the affairs of government, creating a fundamental shift in the paradigm that determines our nation's policies. Those with power and wealth have increasingly learned that, rather than compete, it is much more expedient and profitable to simply buy the control that will ensure success. This is why most all our nation's vital statistics have dramatically worsened over the last 50 years, regardless of which political party has held office. We have failed to update the rules by which our politicians operate, leaving political corruption to become so prevalent and powerful that it now reaches across constitutionally independent branches of government, to accomplish its objectives. This is the underlying reason politics have become increasingly contentious. It reflects the growing frustration that citizens feel with a system that is becoming less and less effective at meeting their needs. All the specious arguing and rhetoric over which political party is to blame is but a noisy distraction keeping us from recognizing and addressing the fundamental problem, an antiquated set of rules that increasingly enable politicians to serve special interests at the expense of the people. This is the why the wealth gap continues to widen, the personal savings rate, which was once in double digits, is now approaching negative numbers, and the next generation is destined to be the first that is financially worse off than their parents. Until we learn that our rules must be perpetually updated to keep the playing field level for all segments of society, by nature, wealth and power will be illicitly drained from the masses and funneled to a limited few, a reality that invariably leads to socioeconomic collapse.

OUR UNRELENTING MIGRATION FROM IRRATIONAL TO RATIONAL BEHAVIORS

When we act on impulse alone, our behaviors are by definition irrational. Only to the extent we consciously intervene between our instinctual promptings to act and our actions are we able to elevate our behaviors from irrational to rational. Accordingly, if we are to advance, both individually and as a species, the fundamental task before us is always one of increasing the mental wherewithal to make such conscious interventions. This is how our behaviors become increasingly tempered and refined. Whether we're trying to control our anger or just eat healthier, our growing awareness enables us to better resist our cruder intrinsically nearsighted instinctual promptings.

Like all forms of life, the human species is a work in progress, an irrationally driven quest to become ever more rational. It's something that can be seen by looking at some of our strongest instinctually driven behaviors, over time. For instance, it's likely not just a coincidence that the physically strongest gender also has the strongest sex drive and can reach orgasm the easiest. In terms of our species' development, it wasn't that long ago when we didn't have such conscious capabilities and relied more on the pairing of such physical traits to ensure reproduction. This is the likely reason a common sexual fantasy of both men and women involves the man having his way with the woman in a rather physical manner. It's an instinctual remnant of that earlier time, when our behaviors were more irrational than rational. The fact that the sexual orientation of women tends to be more *genderdextrous* than that of men is also likely such a remnant. Back when physical dominance played a larger role in mating, while a male's attraction to a female was essential, the inverse did less to ensure procreation, making it a somewhat lesser genetic priority. Though we take it for granted, the fact that we now have laws to ensure that sex be consensual says a great deal about how far we have come in our evolving quest for rationality.

But you also don't have to look very far to see that we still have a long way to go. Perhaps our most shameful example of continuing irrational behavior is the thousands of people we allow to die each year due to a shortage of donated organs. There is no rational logic or reason for not donating one's organs after death, to save someone else's life. Such is the disparity between how we like to perceive ourselves and how we truly are. We like to think of ourselves as an advanced, enlightened, and caring society. Yet we still allow thousands of people to die for no better reason than our irrational fears and imagined pretenses. Again, this is just one of the innumerable ways that, even though it seems innocuous, doing things for imaginary reasons can result in unimaginable harm. Perhaps if everyone could experience firsthand the inexpressible anguish of waiting helplessly at a son or daughter's bedside during their last few days, desperately hoping that an organ will become available, perhaps then we might begin to grasp the enormous unseen costs of our irrational behaviors. Untold numbers of life-saving organs are needlessly destroyed every year for no better reason than our collective ignorance about the things we feel. For anyone interested in becoming a donor, it's as simple and easy as going to organdonor.gov and typing in your name, gender, address, e-mail address, place of birth, and date of birth.

The fact that we are somewhat oblivious to our irrational promptings is why we draw little to no distinction between acquiring knowledge and the ability to employ it. When we teach a child how to do something, we often mistakenly expect that they should then be able to do it. What we fail to recognize is that our ability to perform a task is dependent on more than just knowledge and physical capability. It requires enough awareness to remain rational and deal with unforeseen instinctual promptings in real time, something that takes years to develop. We can teach a young child the safe way to use a lawnmower or fire a gun. But that doesn't mean they'll be capable of doing either safely. To use such things safely, one must be able to incorporate their knowledge amidst a minefield of instinctually triggered compulsions to act without thinking, spontaneous chemical changes that are often able to thwart even the most capable of adults. And the amount of data on childhood accidents that can be attributed to our lack of awareness regarding this reality is staggering.

HOW OUR GROWING AWARENESS IS GRADUALLY DISSOLVING RELIGION

As our awareness grows, knowledge gradually displaces the need to imagine explanations. Because we now understand that plagues, earthquakes, and eclipses are entirely natural events, we no longer feel the need to fabricate supernatural explanations for them. We're also becoming more cognizant of the causal relationship between religion and conflict, which is gradually increasing our scrutiny of the behavior. Because we are getting better at linking our behaviors to their causes and effects, such pretenses of supernatural knowledge are becoming a less attractive source of comfort. Our growing awareness is naturally orchestrating a gradual withdrawal from behaviors of unwarranted comfort and replacing them with behaviors of more purposeful logic and reason. The fact that this country's creators saw fit to keep religion out of government is an extraordinary example at the forefront of this natural progression.

We're also beginning to apprehend and accept that death is but a natural component of the life cycle, which gives us less cause to imagine supernatural scenarios that portray life as continuing. Increasingly, we recognize that life comprises an eclectic assortment of physical elements that are naturally set in motion for an ever so brief snippet of time, an elaborate cascade of energies that nature has choreographed to culminate in their eventual return to a silent solitary place in the universe. The fact that life is a precious and limited continuum of physical events is something our preoccupation with being often prevents us from seeing. But only by grasping this basic reality do we begin to untangle and relinquish the human perplexity that is religion.

More and more people are beginning to recognize what many nonreligious people already know: that it is just as easy, if not easier, to become accustomed to embracing truth and reality, as it is to be conditioned in a pretense of supernatural knowledge, and that, as a result, we can live happier, healthier, more productive, prosperous, and meaningful lives. This psychological shortcut to feeling better will in fact diminish, but only as fast as we become aware of its extraordinary costs, both financial and human.

The question that looms large is whether or not we will gain that awareness in time to avoid a major catastrophe. Will enough people recognize the harm of practicing religion, before an individual or group addicted to its irrationality gets hold of and detonates a chemical, biological, or nuclear weapon? If there is a God, I suspect our relationship with it will not be harmed by us dropping our pretense of knowing the unknowable and humbly living within the limited knowledge we have. To quote Galileo, "I do not feel obliged to believe that the same God who has endowed us with sense, reason, and intellect has intended us to forgo their use."[70] Unfortunately, weighing heavily on our prognosis is the inordinately large number of people who are still looking at a long arduous journey to reach such awareness. Peace cannot occur on a global scale until we each embrace the fact that religion is not knowledge, but rather a significant delusional source of comfort, which is something it seems many people the world over are not yet willing or able to do.

Subconsciously, we are all acutely aware of our self-deceptions, and we increasingly recognize them at the conscious level. Consequently, at some point in the future people will no doubt look back and view our current use of religion and all the harm that it causes in much the same way we view the ritualistic human sacrifices of generations past: as simply the natural result of living during a time of lesser awareness. The pretense of knowledge that we call religion is but another flat Earth that humanity has yet to recognize and put behind it on its inexorable path of increasing awareness. In the words of the 19th-century essayist and poet Ralph Waldo Emerson, "The religion of one age is the literary entertainment of the next."[71]

THE UNRIVALED SIGNIFICANCE OF RATIONAL VS. IRRATIONAL BEHAVIORS

So here we are, seven billion strong in the 21st century. We've come to realize that the Earth is not flat, that we share a majority of our DNA with even the simplest of organisms, and that our universe humbles even the most expansive comprehensions. Yet we still find ourselves involved in horrific conflicts over whose imagined source of comfort is sacrosanct and whose is preposterous. Which begs the simple question: why? What is it that makes us pretend that things we imagine are irrefutable knowledge? Simply put, we are subjective beings that are driven by how we feel, and embracing such a pretense can make us feel better. Again, this is what makes being truthful with ourselves so inherently difficult. Even though we need truth to survive, attaining it often requires that we resist nature's urge to feel better in the moment.

The conscious capability to selectively override our genetic responses to the environment represents nature's most significant and beneficial development. If we are to condition our children in any behavior, it should not be to escape reality when it makes them uncomfortable, but rather to confront those discomforts in a rational manner. The strongest causations of beneficial and harmful behaviors are rational and irrational thoughts, respectively. We know that a good education can greatly benefit our children over the course of their lives, but it seems we have yet to recognize just how much we can help them before they ever reach school. By implanting the propensity to remain rational, we can dramatically enhance a child's ability to learn and achieve, regardless of what path they take.

As conscious beings, we continuously struggle to employ lucid thought amidst a continuum of emotions, to reap the benefits of a more measured response. Whether it's the hatred of racism, the unwarranted hope of politics, or the unrealistic certainty decreed in religious texts, the human struggle is never between such imagined forces as good and evil or God and the Devil, but rather always between rationality and irrationality. We can either arrive at purposeful behaviors through logic and reason, or we can simply act on our emotions and be forced to forever rationalize. The ability to effect rational behaviors is what separates our current world of conflict and hatred from one of peace and cooperation. When we fail to require credible substantiation in discerning the real from the unreal, we forego the ability to make rational decisions and engage in rational behaviors, which is precisely how and why religion generates so much harm.

Contrary to conventional thinking, the root cause of any religious conflict is not a particular religion or how its originating text is worded. It is the more basic fact that humans must become irrational to practice religion. This is why the bloodshed caused by nonreligious leaders such as Stalin or Mao, though substantial, is but a drop in the bucket when compared to that caused by religious leaders. While only a portion of nonreligious behaviors are irrational, the very nature of religion necessitates that everything done in its name be done for irrational reasons.

Our technical knowledge, that which reflects the rational side of human behavior, is doubling every couple of years. Yet our understanding of why we practice religion, the only irrational behavior we not only tolerate but embrace and encourage, has remained virtually unchanged throughout history. The immense significance being, only by understanding and curbing our irrational behaviors are we able to mitigate the rapidly growing dangers that accompany our soaring awareness. This is why new technologies, such as nuclear energy, the Internet, and our burgeoning ability to alter genetic instructions, are received with both anticipation and apprehension, as both a blessing and a curse. Because science is a morally neutral discipline, latent in every new innovation is the potential for both benefit and harm, potential that grows ever larger and makes life ever more tenuous as we become more aware.

14

Twelve Elemental Truths and the Global Peace That Awaits Their Recognition

The 19th-century politician, educational reformer, and abolitionist Horace Mann once said, "Be ashamed to die until you have won some victory for humanity."[72] It is in that spirit that I offer the following twelve realities of nature, awareness that is needed for peaceful coexistence. Only when these twelve truths become knowledge as common as that of our planet's shape will humanity purge itself of the errant perspectives that generate our most horrific conflicts. Only then will we become immune to being manipulated through our emotions and imaginary panaceas, to commit atrocities in defense of things we can only pretend to know. Only then will the human race, for the first time, find itself in a relative state of world peace.

1) **Our knowledge is limited by nature to physical things and events.** Because our awareness is derived exclusively through our senses, and our senses can only detect physical phenomena, everything in and about the human experience, including our innermost thoughts and feelings, consists entirely of physical matter being moved about by

physical energies. Consequently, there are no legitimate uses for terms such as truth, knowledge, fact, certainty, or belief when it comes to religion or anything else deemed to be nonphysical or supernatural. Despite any and all claims to the contrary, when it comes to God, heaven, or any kind of afterlife, every human being knows exactly as much as every other: absolutely nothing at all.

2) **Our feelings are the means by which our genetic instructions prompt and guide our behaviors.** Human life is, like every other form of life, a series of genetically induced reactions to the environment, the sole purpose of which is to effect survival. The chemical changes that initiate and steer those reactions are what we consciously recognize as our feelings and emotions. This is how and why everything we think, say, and do has a natural origin and purpose: they are always preceded by genetically triggered chemical changes. Our conscious faculties do not preclude these genetic promptings, but rather occur downstream of and are subservient to them, so as to temper and refine the behaviors they produce. The fact that our feelings represent our most primal form of guidance is what makes us subjective, emotionally fragile creatures.

3) **There is no such thing as a selfless behavior.** Because every behavior of every living thing is genetically initiated to enhance survival, by nature, everything we feel, think, say, and do is necessarily for the purpose of benefitting ourselves.

4) **We are genetically instructed to obtain benefit both individually and jointly.** The trait that differentiates social animals from all the rest of life is an instinctual impulsion to exhibit behaviors that facilitate coexistence. This is how

seemingly selfless behaviors provide benefit. When we help others, it doesn't just satisfy our innate need for acceptance, it facilitates the considerable benefits that can be achieved by living and working together.

5) **Our values and morality are but manifestations of the social behaviors that we perceive provide benefit.** Good behavior is, by definition, that which benefits the group (i.e., social behavior). We naturally and necessarily exhibit such behaviors when we perceive them as providing more benefit than individual behaviors. This is why religious people behave no better than the nonreligious. The consideration we show others is a product of our innate desire to coexist, an instinctual need that is common to everyone.

6) **We determine truth and reality instinctively at the subconscious level.** Because our survival depends on us discerning that which is true and real in our environment, long before we attained our conscious capabilities, our genetic instructions developed an unconscious method of deriving that information from the physical things our senses detect. We are now able to contribute conscious input to that unconscious process, but only if and to the extent our circumstances are conducive to refinements in our behavior.

7) **The process of consciously choosing is actually one of realizing instinctual determinations that have already been made at the subconscious level.** Because everything we think, say, and do is prompted and guided by genetic responses to the things we encounter, our conscious choices are always a byproduct of those preconscious determinations.

8) **Our beliefs are but a manifestation of the things we instinctually determine to be true and real.** Our beliefs represent our conscious awareness of the feelings of confidence and certainty, feelings that are naturally, necessarily, and instantaneously triggered by those preconscious determinations. This is why we have absolutely no say in the things we believe. The feelings they represent have already been produced by the time we become aware of them.

9) **By nature, mankind comprises only atheists and agnostics.** Because our beliefs are but a conscious representation of our instinctual determinations, which are entirely derived from the things we detect with our senses, they cannot and do not materialize regarding anything that isn't physical in nature. Our complete absence of nonphysical experiences can result in a belief that there is no God, which would make one an atheist. Realizing that we have no means to become aware of the nonphysical can result in a belief that we cannot know, which would make one an agnostic. But it is a categorical reality that there is nothing among our entirely physical experiences that can or does trigger a belief in the nonphysical, making the notion of a religious belief perhaps our most prominent self-delusion.

10) **Religion does not improve human behavior.** Because our genetic instructions have evolved to effect our survival by taking advantage of recurring phenomena in the environment, they have come to rely on the physical things we actually experience and not the things we merely imagine. Because it produces no repeatable effects, the notion of anything supernatural is entirely irrelevant to the genetic processes that determine our behaviors.

11) **Conflict is intrinsic to religion.** Because human beings are devoid of knowledge regarding the supernatural, and we cannot apply logic and reason to things of which we have no knowledge, religion must be entirely imagined, and is therefore conjecture, at best. And because no two people ever imagine the exact same thing, no matter how much it might appear that we agree on "what God wants," such creations of the mind always necessarily conflict not just with reality, but with everyone else's unique such creations. The reason religious conflicts can be so horrific is that those unique creations serve to ease some of our greatest instinctual discomforts, but only to the extent we embrace and defend them as ultimate knowledge.

12) **Latent in even the most innocuous forms of religion is the potential for unthinkable harm.** Because religion requires that we reject reason and deny reality, to the degree we become conditioned in its practice, we become at the mercy of our emotions and subject to manipulation. At best, we endorse the irrationality that enables destruction on a massive scale. At worst, we make ourselves vulnerable to those who would exploit our irrationality to accomplish genocidal endeavors.

In the words of Albert Einstein, "Peace cannot be kept by force. It can only be achieved by understanding."[73] Humanity can exist contently side by side, but only if it culls the untruths and irrational behaviors that propagate large-scale conflicts, the very things religion excels in creating. Peace hinges not on getting others to see things as we do, but rather on everyone seeing things as they actually are, something that requires a rational mindset.

Everyone wants to live in a world at peace, but so far relatively few people are willing or able to endure the discomforting truths required to achieve it. Such is the current state of human awareness. Until we begin to grasp the enormity of the damage we are causing with the practice of religion, we are destined to do nothing more than grow tired and sickened by the inexorable carnage it leaves in its wake. Until we each recognize that inherent in any pretense of supernatural knowledge is the capacity for unspeakable harm, and begin to own that reality in our own lives, we will continue contributing to this global irrationality and the devastation it propagates.

15

A Footnote of Sorts about Our Subjective Perspective

If many of the things you read here seem a bit surprising, harsh, cynical, or otherwise uncomfortable to embrace, it's important to recognize that this is a natural effect of a subjective perspective. Because we are subjective beings and our most elemental pursuit is always comfort, we never interpret our experiences with total objectivity. We always contort our experiences to some degree to make them better fit our existing perspective, a perspective that by nature embodies our emotional wants and needs.

When you read things in this book that differed from your current understanding, you unconsciously sought ways to question, doubt, or otherwise discredit them in a natural attempt to sustain your existing perspective. That's what we necessarily do as subjective beings. We invariably see things not as they are, but more like we wish them to be, and then try to defend that perspective. Hence the phrase "the truth hurts." That hurt is the discomfort we feel when our naturally distorted perspective is confronted by reality. But then again, as the ancient Greek philosopher Diogenes of Sinope, who lived in the 4th century BC, wrote, "Of what use is a philosopher who doesn't hurt anybody's feelings?"[74]

Notes

1. Johann Georg Hamann and James C. O'Flaherty, *Hamann's Socratic Memorabilia: A Translation and Commentary* (Baltimore: Johns Hopkins Press, 1967), 147.

2. Kees W. Bolle, *Secrecy in Religions* (Leiden: E.J. Brill, 1987), 143.

3. Larry Chang, *Wisdom for the Soul: Five Millennia of Prescriptions for Spiritual Healing* (Washington, DC: Gnosophia Publishers, 2006), 698.

4. Thomas Paine and H. D. Symonds, *Common Sense: Addressed to the Inhabitants of America, on the Following Interesting Subjects: I. Of the Origin and Design of Government in general, with concise Remarks on the English Constitution. II. Of Monarchy and Hereditary Succession. III. Thoughts on the present State of American Affairs. IV. Of the present Ability of America, with some miscellaneous Reflections* (London: Printed for H.D. Symonds, Paternoster-Row, 1792), 43.

5. Daniel R. Schwarz, *Disraeli's Fiction* (New York: The Macmillan Press Ltd., 1979), 41.

6. P.T. Barnum, Barrypopik.com, August 25, 2011. http://www.barrypopik.com/index.php/new_york_city/entry/if_you_want_to_build_a_crowd_start_a_fight, accessed January 7, 2017.

7. Darnell M. Hunt, *O.J. Simpson Facts and Fictions: News Rituals in the Construction of Reality* (Cambridge, UK: Cambridge University Press, 1999), 19.

8. Margaret S. Clark and Judson Mills, "Interpersonal attraction in exchange and communal relationships" *Journal of Personality and Social Psychology* 37, no. 1 (1979): 12-24. doi:10.1037//0022-3514.37.1.12.

9. Daniel Weis, *Everlasting Wisdom* (Place of publication not identified: Paragon Publishing, 2010), 78.

10. Dean Kalahar, *Blind Perceptions: Sociopolitical Psychology and its Impact on Civilization* (New York: IUniverse, 2005), 2.

11. Thomas R. Rosebrough and Ralph Geist Leverett, *Transformational Teaching in the Information Age: Making Why and How We Teach Relevant to Students* (Alexandria, Virginia USA: ASCD, 2011), 137.

12. Joseph C. Lundwall, *The Truth About Prayer and Divine Revelation* (Raleigh: Lulu Publishing Services, 2014), 106.

13. Mark Hallett, "Volitional control of movement: The physiology of free will" *Clinical Neurophysiology* Vol. 118, Issue 6 (2007): 1179-1192. doi: 10.1016/j.clinph.2007.03.019.

14. U.S. Department of Justice, Federal Bureau of Investigation, Criminal Justice Information Services Division (2015), *Crime In The United States, Expanded Homicide Data Table 15, Justifiable Homicide by Weapon, Private Citizen, 2011-2015.*

15. CDC, National Vital Statistics Reports (NVSS) Vol. 64, No. 2, Table 18: *Deaths: Final Data for 2013.* (February 16, 2016): 84.

16. Charles Rex Arbogast, *Justice Scalia defends comparing sodomy ban to murder ban* Associated press, Dec 11, 2012.

17. Mark Twain and Caroline Thomas Harnsberger, *Mark Twain at Your Fingertips: A Book of Quotations* (New York: Cloud, Inc., 1948), 425.

18. David Hume and Andrew Millar, *Four dissertations: I. the Natural History of Religion. II. of the Passions. III. of Tragedy. IV. of the Standard of Taste* (London: Printed for A. Millar, in the Strand, 1757), 83.

19. John Heywood, Actualfreedom.com, 2017. http://www.actualfreedom.com.au/richard/abditorium/nonesoblind.htm, accessed January 7, 2017.

20. Ambrose Bierce, *The Collected Works of Ambrose Bierce* (New York: Neale, 1911), 261.

21. Thomas Paine, *The Political Writings of Thomas Paine: Secretary to the Committee of Foreign Affairs in the American Revolution: To Which Is Prefixed a Brief Sketch of the Author's Life* (Charlestown (Ms.): G. Davidson, 1824), 284.

22. Ethan Allen, *Reason, the Only Oracle of Man: or, A Compenduous System of Natural Religion* (Boston: Mendum, Cornhill, 1854), 72.

23. Mark Twain, *The wit and wisdom of Mark Twain: A Book of Quotations* (Mineola, NY: Dover Publications, 1999), 26.

24. Will M. Gervais and Ara Norenzayan, "Analytic Thinking Promotes Religious Disbelief" *Science* 336, no. 6080 (2012): 493-96. doi:10.1126/science.1215647.

25. Miron Zuckerman, Jordan Silberman, and Judith A. Hall, "The Relation Between Intelligence and Religiosity: A Meta-Analysis and Some Proposed Explanations" *Personality and Social Psychology Review* 17, no. 4 (2013): 325-54. doi:10.1177/1088868313497266.

26. Win-gallop international, "Global Index of Religiosity and Atheism – 2012." News release.

27. Steve Wilkens, Craig A. Boyd, Alan G. Padgett, and Carl A. Raschke, *Faith and Reason: Three Views*, (Downers Grove, IL: InterVarsity Press, 2014), 13.

28. Malieth Tonnerre, *The Future Affects The Past: What Destination is Time Rushing to?* (Place of publication not identified: Red Lead Books, 2013), 14.

29. Daniel C. Dennett, *Breaking the Spell: Religion as a Natural Phenomenon* (New York: Viking, 2006), 17.

30. Noson S. Yanofsky, *The Outer Limits of Reason: What Science, Mathematics, and Logic Cannot Tell Us* (Cambridge, MA: The MIT Press, 2013), 345.

31. Michael Shermer, *Why People Believe Weird Things: Pseudoscience, Superstition, and Other Confusions of Our Time* (New York: W.H. Freeman, 1997), 43.

32. Seth Borenstein, NBCnews.com, November 4, 2013. http://www.nbcnews.com/science/8-8-billion-habitable-earth-size-planets-exist-milky-way-8C11529186, accessed January 12, 2017.

33. E. Christopher Reyes, *In His Name*, Vol. III, (Place of publication not identified: Trafford Publishing, 2014), 210.

34. Charles T. Sprading, *Liberty and the Great Libertarians: An Anthology on Liberty, A Hand-book of Freedom* (New York: Arno Press, 1972), 206.

35. Thomas Jefferson and Paul Leicester Ford, *The Works of Thomas Jefferson* (New York: Cosimo Classics, 2009).

36. Voltaire, BrainyQuote.com, Xplore Inc, 2017. https://www.brainyquote.com/quotes/quotes/v/voltaire118641.html, accessed January 5, 2017.

37. Chamberlain Research Consultants (1994), *Survey Re: "In God We Trust"* Madison, WI.

38. Thomas Jefferson and H. A. Washington, *The Writings of Thomas Jefferson: Being His Autobiography, Correspondence, Reports, Messages, Addresses, and Other Writings, Official and Private. Published by the Order of the Joint Committee of Congress on the Library, from the Original Manuscripts, Deposited in the Department of State* (Washington, D.C.: Taylor & Maury, 1853), 239.

39. Mark Twain and Frederick Anderson, *Mark Twain's Notebooks & Journals* (Berkeley: Univ. of Calif. P., 1975), 305.

40. Carter Godwin Woodson, *The Mis-education of the Negro* (Place of publication not identified: Clearwords.org, 2009), 61.

41. James A. Haught, *2000 Years of Disbelief: Famous People with the Courage to Doubt* (Amherst, NY: Prometheus Books, 1996), 201.

42. Robert A. Nowlan, *The American Presidents from Polk to Hayes: What They Did, What They Said and What Was Said About Them* (Denver, CO: Outskirts Press, 2016), 228.

43. John S. C. Abbott, *Napoleon at St. Helena; or, Interesting Anecdotes and Remarkable Conversations of the Emperor During the Five and a Half Years of His Captivity* (New York: Harper & Brothers, 1855), 245.

44. Penny Edgell, Joseph Gerteis, and Douglas Hartmann, "Atheists As 'Other': Moral Boundaries and Cultural Membership in American Society" *American Sociological Review* 71, no. 2 (2006): 211-34. doi:10.1177/000312240607100203.

45. The Critic Company, *The Critic*, Vol. 47, No. 1, (New Rochelle: G. P. Putnam's Sons, 1905), 111.

46. Bernard Spilka, Ralph W. Hood, and Richard L. Gorsuch, *The Psychology of Religion: An Empirical Approach* (New York: Guilford Press, 2003), 281.

47. Federal Bureau of Prisons (2014), *Survey Re: Prisoner Religious Affiliation*. Washington, DC.

48. Edd Doerr, (1987). Bashing public education, *Humanist*, Vol. 47 issue 4, Jul/Aug 1987, 43.

49. Jean Decety, Jason M. Cowell, Kang Lee, Randa Mahasneh, Susan Malcolm-Smith, Bilge Selcuk, and Xinyue Zhou, "The Negative Association between Religiousness and Children's Altruism across the World" *Current Biology* 25, no. 22 (2015): 2951-955. doi:10.1016/j.cub.2015.09.056.

50. Samuel S. Janus and Cynthia L. Janus, *The Janus Report on Sexual Behavior* (New York: John Wiley & Sons, 1993).

51. Deborah L. Hall, David C. Matz, and Wendy Wood, "Why Don't We Practice What We Preach? A Meta-Analytic Review of Religious Racism" *Personality and Social Psychology Review* 14, no. 1 (2010): 126-39. doi:10.1177/1088868309352179.

52. Robert W. Griffiths, *Slaying the Dragon: An Everyman's Rejection of God and Religion* (Tal-y-bont: Y Lolfa, 2012), Chapter 10.

53. George A. Erickson, *Time Traveling with Science and the Saints* (Amherst, NY: Prometheus Books, 2003), 56.

54. Laird M. Wilcox and John H. George, *Be Reasonable: Selected Quotations for Inquiring Minds* (Buffalo, NY: Prometheus Books, 1994), 182.

55. Mark Twain, BrainyQuote.com, Xplore Inc, 2017. https://www.brainyquote.com/quotes/quotes/m/marktwain109624.html, accessed January 5, 2017.

56. James A. Haught, *2000 Years of Disbelief: Famous People with the Courage to Doubt* (Amherst, NY: Prometheus Books, 1996), 65.

57. Steven Weinberg, *Slaying the Dragon: An Everyman's Rejection of God and Religion* (Tal-y-bont: Y Lolfa, 2012), Chapter 10.

58. Harvey J. Kaye, *Thomas Paine and the Promise of America* (New York: Hill and Wang, 2005), 58.

59. Fred R. Shapiro, *The Yale Book of Quotations* (New Haven: Yale University Press, 2006), 325.

60. Emily Dickinson and R. W. Franklin, *The Poems of Emily Dickinson* (Cambridge, MA: Belknap Press, 1999), 627.

61. Bridger Daquan, *American's War Against Human Rights And Justice: "Reason In Religion Is Of Unlawful Use"--Thomas Jefferson* (Victoria, B.C., Canada: Trafford Pub., 2008), Chapter V.

62. Paul-Henri Thiry Holbach and David M. Holohan, *Christianity unveiled* (Surrey, U.K.: Hodgson Press, 2008), 309.

63. Karen Frazier Romero, *The Universal Church of Man* (Place of publication not identified: K. F. Romero, 2015), Chapter Five.

64. Mike King and Linus Roache, *Luminous: The Spiritual Life on Film.* (United States: McFarland & Co, 2014), 219.

65. Heritage Foundation, *Total Welfare Spending Is Rising Despite Attempts at Reform*. Federal spending chart 12. Federal Budget in Pictures 2012.

66. David B. Muhlhausen and Patrick Tyrrell, *The 2013 Index of Dependence on Government* Heritage Foundation Special Report #142. Nov 21, 2013.

67. David W. Moore, *Three in Four Americans Believe in Paranormal* Gallup News Service. Jun 16, 2005.

68. Ben Henderson, *Belief in evolution up since 2004* YouGov Omnibus Poll, Jul 8-9, 2013.

69. Jack Adler, *Splendid Seniors: Great Lives, Great Deeds* (Nashville, TN: Pearlsong Press, 2007), 24.

70. Phil Mundt, *A Scientific Search for Religious Truth* (Austin, TX: Bridgeway Books, 2007), 49.

71. Ralph Waldo Emerson, *Lectures and Biographical Sketches* (Boston: Houghton Mifflin and Company, 1904), 105.

72. Barbie Zelizer, *Making the University Matter* (Abingdon, Oxon: Routledge, 2011), 123.

73. Srinibas Bhattacharya, *Foundations of Education* (New Delhi, India: Atlantic, 2000), 95.

74. Steven Stavropoulos, *The Beginning of All Wisdom: Timeless Advice from the Ancient Greeks* (New York: Marlowe & Co., 2003), 150.

List of Quotes

Allen, Ethan

- "In those parts of the world where learning and science has prevailed, miracles have ceased; but in such parts of it as are barbarous and ignorant, miracles are still in vogue."

Arouet, Francois-Marie (a.k.a. Voltaire)

- "Those who can make you believe absurdities can make you commit atrocities."

Barnum, Phineas Taylor (a.k.a. P.T. Barnum)

- "If you want to draw a crowd, start a fight."

Bayle, Pierre

- "In matters of religion, it is very easy to deceive a man, and very hard to undeceive him."

Beyle, Marie-Henri (a.k.a. Stendhal)

- "All religions are founded on the fear of the many and the cleverness of the few."

Bierce, Ambrose (in his DEVIL'S DICTIONARY, under the word pray)

- "To ask that the laws of the universe be annulled in behalf of a single petitioner confessedly unworthy."

Bonaparte, Napoleon

- "I am surrounded by priests who repeat incessantly that their kingdom is not of this world, and yet they lay their hands on everything they can get."

Buchanan, James (President)

- "I have seldom met an intelligent person whose views were not narrowed and distorted by religion."

Bunuel, Luis

- "God and Country make an unbeatable team; they break all records for oppression and bloodshed."

Byron, George Gordon (a.k.a. Lord Byron)

- "Of religion I know nothing – at least, in its favor."

The Unspoken Truth About Religion

Carus, Titus Lucretius

- "All religions are equally sublime to the ignorant, useful to the politician, and ridiculous to the philosopher."

Clemens, Samuel Langhorne (a.k.a. Mark Twain)

- "Faith is believing what you know ain't so."

- "There is nothing more awe-inspiring than a miracle except the credulity that can take it at par."

- "Religion consists in a set of things which the average man thinks he believes, and wishes he was certain of."

- "It ain't what you don't know that gets you into trouble. It's what you know for sure that just ain't so."

Dickinson, Emily

- "That it will never come again is what makes life so sweet."

Diderot, Denis

- "The philosopher has never killed any priests, whereas the priest has killed a great many philosophers."

Diogenes of Sinope

- "Of what use is a philosopher who doesn't hurt anybody's feelings?"

Disraeli, Benjamin

- "Never apologize for showing feeling. . . when you do so, you apologize for the truth."

Edison, Thomas

- "All Bibles are man-made."

Einstein, Albert

- "A society's competitive advantage will come not from how well its schools teach the multiplication and periodic tables, but from how well they stimulate imagination and creativity."

- "All our science, measured against reality, is primitive and childlike — and yet it is the most precious thing we have."

- "Peace cannot be kept by force; it can only be achieved by understanding."

Emerson, Ralph Waldo

- "A friend is one before whom I may think aloud."

- "The religion of one age is the literary entertainment of the next."

France, Anatole

- "If 50 million people say a foolish thing, it is still a foolish thing."

Fromm, Erich

- "Once a doctrine, however irrational, has gained power in a society, millions of people will believe it rather than feel ostracized and isolated."

Galilei, Galileo

- "You cannot teach a man anything; you can only help him to find it within himself."

- "I do not feel obliged to believe that the same God who has endowed us with sense, reason, and intellect has intended us to forgo their use."

Grellet, Stephen

- "I expect to pass through this world but once. Any good thing therefore that I can do, or any kindness that I can show to any fellow creature, let me do it now. Let me not defer or neglect it, for I shall not pass this way again."

Hamann, Johann Georg

- "A thirsty ambition for truth and virtue, and a frenzy to conquer all lies and vices which are not recognized as such nor desire to be; herein consists the heroic spirit of the philosopher."

Heywood, John

- "There are none so blind as those who will not see. The most deluded people are those who choose to ignore what they already know."

Hitler, Adolf

- "I believe that I am acting in accordance with the will of the Almighty Creator: by defending myself against the Jew, I am fighting for the work of the Lord."

- "I have followed [the Catholic Church] in giving our party program the character of unalterable finality, like the Creed. The Church has realized that anything and everything can be built up on a document of that sort, no matter how contradictory or irreconcilable with it. The faithful will swallow it whole, so long as logical reasoning is never allowed to be brought to bear on it."

- "I am only doing what the Church has done for fifteen hundred years, only more effectively."

Hume, David

- "Men dare not avow, even to their own hearts, the doubts which they entertain on such subjects."

Jefferson, Thomas (President)

- "To compel a man to furnish contributions of money for the propagation of opinions which he disbelieves and abhors, is sinful and tyrannical."

- "Question with boldness even the existence of a God; because, if there be one, he must more approve of the homage of reason, than that of blindfolded fear."

Luther, Martin

- "Reason is the greatest enemy that faith has; it never comes to the aid of spiritual things, but — more frequently than not — struggles against the divine Word, treating with contempt all that emanates from God."

Mann, Horace

- "Be ashamed to die until you have won some victory for humanity."

Montaigne, Michel de

- "[Man] cannot make a worm, yet he will make gods by the dozen."

Newton, Isaac (a.k.a. Sir Isaac Newton)

- "A man may imagine things that are false, but he can only understand things that are true."

- "If I have seen further, it is by standing on the shoulders of giants."

- "What we know is a drop, what we don't know is an ocean."

Paine, Thomas

- "He who takes nature for his guide is not easily beaten out of his argument."

- "It is error only, and not truth, that shrinks from inquiry."

- "Tis dearness only that gives everything its value."

Seneca, Lucius Annaeus

- "Religion is regarded by the common people as true, by the wise as false, and by rulers as useful."

Thoreau, Henry David

- "I did not see why the schoolmaster should be taxed to support the priest, and not the priest the schoolmaster."

Weinberg, Steven

- "With or without religion you would have good people doing good things and evil people doing evil things. But for good people to do evil things, that takes religion."

Woodson, Carter G, Ph.D.

- "Practically all the incompetents and undesirables who have been barred from other walks of life by race prejudice and economic difficulties have rushed into the ministry for the exploitation of the people."

Made in the USA
Columbia, SC
20 May 2018